GOING... GOING...
ANECDOTES OF A WELSH AUCTIONEER

er budd

in aid of

AMBIWLANS AWYR CYMRU
WALES AIR AMBULANCE

4721800000404 7

Going... Going...

ANECDOTES OF A WELSH AUCTIONEER

David Rogers Jones

Acknowledgments

I wish to thank all those who have lent their treasured photographs for the book – Mrs Gwyneth Owen, Mr Iolo Owen and Mrs Sally-Ann Williams and for their consent to use them.

To Margaret, my wife and to Shân, our daughter, for supplementing my very limited computing skills!

To Myrddin ap Dafydd of Gwasg Carreg Gwalch, Llanrwst for his expertise, advice and encouragement.

First published in 2014

© David Rogers Jones

© Gwasg Carreg Gwalch 2014

The royalties of this book will be paid to
Ambiwlans Awyr Cymru
Wales Air Ambulance

ISBN: 978-1-84524-231-2

Cover design: Eleri Owen

Published by Gwasg Carreg Gwalch,
12 Iard yr Orsaf, Llanrwst, Wales LL26 0EH
tel: 01492 642031
email: books@carreg-gwalch.com
internet: www.carreg-gwalch.com

To my Mother
whose idea it was in the first place.

Wales Air Ambulance/
Ambiwlans Awyr Cymru

Proceeds from the sale of this book will be donated to one of Wales' most worthy causes – the Wales Air Ambulance Service which covers the whole of the Principality from its centres in Caernarfon, Welshpool and Swansea.

Countless numbers of families and individuals have reason to be forever grateful for a service which provides such quick response to urgent and accidental situations throughout Wales.

Every operational take-off costs the service a minimum of £1500 so the importance of volunteer funding cannot be over emphasised.

I hope you enjoy my book, the sale of which will help, in a small way, a very worthy and valuable cause. And if you have enjoyed it, try not to be tempted to pass it on to friends but to suggest they buy their own!

David Rogers Jones

AMBIWLANS AWYR CYMRU
WALES AIR AMBULANCE

Contents

1 In the Beginning 1960–1963   9

2 Caernarfon 1963–1967   61

3 Harlech and Hereford 1967–1968   75

4 Anglesey 1968–1992   86

5 Colwyn Bay 1992   128

1

In The Beginning
1960–1963

Childhood in Llandudno Junction in the austerity years of the 1950s was, quite simply, a lovely uncomplicated doddle. Maelgwyn Primary School with its impressive headmaster O. M. Roberts was a haven of unbridled happiness and he, together with an excellent team of teachers, gave me five years of relatively easy achievement.

I remember the sheer charisma of our fifth form master, Emyr Roberts of Betws-y-coed who, seemingly always on a Monday morning, regaled us all with his weekend's exploits

Ysgol Maelgwn school soccer champions 1952-1953.
Yours truly top row right.

with the fishing rods at his beloved Llyn Elsi above Betws village. There was lovely Gwilym Parry who had enlisted into the teaching profession straight from war service. Handsome Gwilym was in charge of sports, amongst other things, and if you were good enough to be a member of the school football team which I was (left wing), your leisure-time happiness at Maelgwyn was guaranteed. Then there was the strict (the very, very strict) Miss Owen or, as she was more commonly referred to, Miss Owen Barnsley. How the Yorkshire town name became attached to hers I know not, but my memory of her was that of a very strict disciplinarian. Ian Botham would have been very envious of her prowess as a thrower. Not, I hasten to add, as a thrower of a cricket ball, but as a very lethal thrower of a piece of chalk in the direction of any pupil perceived by her to be misbehaving. She never, ever, missed!

The year 1955 saw me take my 11-plus exams for entry into John Bright Grammar School in Llandudno. As I recall, there was no homework regime at Maelgwyn to speak of, but this did not hinder my very easy passage to John Bright and to the second stage of my educational career. My 11-plus result put me straight into the A stream at John Bright. To the reader, this might sound extremely boastful, but my come-uppance was very quickly to be delivered to me with the realisation, forcefully pointed out to me and fellow pupils by the very experienced band of teachers that homework, and lots of it, was to be accepted very much as the norm if we were not to be left behind in a regime that, quite clearly, would leave us stranded and well behind in the educational pecking order.

It became very clear that the leap from what had been for me such an easy and relaxed regime at Maelgwyn would help me not one little bit at John Bright. This, after all, was the highly-respected conventional grammar school which was to turn out future politicians, chief constables, scientists and successful self-employed business people. It had little time for those who chose not to put in the required hours of hard graft and study. One single term of relative inactivity of the extra-curricular kind soon convinced my superiors that I was not, after all, of the required A-stream material. The result, to the disgust of my parents, was swift and simple – demotion to the B stream.

As far as school holidays were concerned I have to state, in my defence, that I did apply myself rather more fruitfully to the tasks in hand. One of my regular 'pocket money jobs' was to report on a casual basis to my father's dispensing chemist shop in Llandudno Junction to be given medicines for delivery on my bike to those customers in the locality who had left their prescriptions in the queue for my father to deal with.

I remember so well my father's pride in having the Lord and Lady Aberconwy of Bodnant Hall as his customers and that on occasions it became my duty, after school, to ride to Bodnant with a completed 'script,' as they were referred to. But it was my father's word-for-word exhortation that I remember so clearly. "Don't forget when you arrive there to go through the rear yard to the tradesmen's entrance." My father had the irrational fear that his delivery boy would ride up to the front door with his bike just like our local paper delivery boy in the Junction. Old-fashioned class distinction?

My father also had one other 'prestigious' customer in the locality – Liverpool Corporation – which owned, and ran, Woodland School, an establishment for 'under-performing' boys. As a deliverer of prescription medicines to the school, I became familiar with the layout of the premises and also with the location and potential of a lovely apple orchard which was part of the complex.

Two friends and I decided one day, that we would relieve some of the trees of their delicious bounty. We had not been trespassing very long before we suddenly realised that we had company in the form of the very feared and impressive Sergeant Owen, the local Junction bobby. We were quickly and very effectively subjected to an extremely loud and quite fearsome telling-off and warned as to our future conduct. As far as the sergeant was concerned, an hour of his time had been wasted so he was less than pleased with our conduct.

My problem was a big one – I had effectively been the instigator of what is known today in criminal circles as an 'inside job', If the story got back to my father – a more than likely possibility as the local police house was only a short distance from the shop – I would be in deep trouble and, more importantly, my father would fear the loss of Liverpool Corporation as his customers! Fortunately for me nothing further was said or done, thus bringing my short criminal career to an end.

During my last two years at John Bright, the summer holidays saw me land what I regarded as an extremely prestigious holiday job. I cannot recall exactly how the introduction came about but I somehow found myself being interviewed at Junction railway station for the post of 'junior porter' which basically involved waving a red flag and getting very well paid for doing so! To clarify, the job involved quite a degree of responsibility at Llandudno Junction Crossing where, in those days, the Junction to Llandudno branch line crossed the main road leading from the Junction to Conwy via the Cob. The railway crossing had a pair of manually-operated gates which required their opening for every train that passed through. In those days train was very much 'king', to the extent that the Llandudno Branch was extremely busy with special excursions taking day trippers and holidaymakers to and from the lovely resort.

What used to happen operationally, was that the signalman in the box overlooking the crossing would give a shout to indicate that a train was imminent, whereupon it became my task to step out, wave the red flag and stop the traffic preparatory to closing the gates. The degree of false importance which that red flag gave was quite unbelievable but the Powers That Be must have been sufficiently satisfied with my performance to offer me the job on a similar basis during the following year's Summer holidays. Railway nostalgia buffs will doubtless recall that the exact location of the crossing gates, which gave me such pleasureable and remunerative summer holidays, was exactly opposite the present main doors of the Crosville depot which has overlooked such major road works and fly-over changes as to render the area barely recognizable today.

Much as I had enjoyed my Summer job, I think I was sufficiently savvy to realise that any future as a flag-waving junior porter had its limitations and that very soon I had to be giving serious thought as to what lay ahead of me by way of a 'proper' career, as one's parents might say. The main problem was that whilst I shone reasonably well at John Bright on the sporting side – left wing in the School's first soccer team – my educational efforts and aspirations were ordinary to say the least.

Before I barely had time to realise it, the challenge of O levels was suddenly upon me and some really serious graft was going to be required if complete ignominy were to be avoided.

I do not remember the build-up to those important exams except to be able to state that at the first effort I achieved seven passes and stayed on another term to re-sit, and pass, an eighth subject. Which one that was, I cannot recall, which says little for my enthusiasm at the time! Today's O level student may well adjudge eight O levels as a reasonable achievement but this is not how the teaching hierarchy of John Bright Grammar School would have viewed such ordinary efforts in 1960! The end result was that I left John Bright in the summer of 1960 without ceremony or rancour, but without knowing precisely where my first step in a career path was to take me.

Mother Pops the Question

So there I was nearing the end of summer 1959, with no really firm ideas in mind as to how I might join the world of the paid worker. I had committed myself to a departure from John Bright with no regrets whatsoever, not that remaining at the school had been a realistic alternative anyway.

I was aware that somewhere in the background my parents, particularly my mother, had ideas that a career 'in the bank' might be just up my street, although suggestions and ideas were not exactly bouncing off the walls. It was true at that time that anyone with a little bit about them had a very good chance of making a good career 'in the bank'. A particular reason was that the banking sector at the time was experiencing high numbers of retiring managers, which, coupled with other financial and other commercial reasons, made a career in banking a very attractive prospect.

It took me far less time to flatly turn down 'the bank' than it had taken my parents to come round to making the firm suggestion that this might be my future career path. Back to square one then! Some days passed without any further career suggestions in the offing, when suddenly, out of the blue one day mother asked how I might fancy becoming an auctioneer! I knew immediately how this idea had come about. Mother was quite an avid auction-goer having not only attended, but bought at, several auctions held at quality residences in and around the Colwyn Bay area in the 1950s. She had acquired a decent knowledge of the subject and a few nice pieces in the house were testament to her obvious enthusiasm.

It transpired that at that precise time, an advert had appeared in the local newspaper seeking a pupil auctioneer at a firm in nearby Bangor and eagle-eyed mother had spotted this. The firm was John Pritchard and Company owned and run, by Mr Ronald Mackenzie. With slightly less enthusiasm than my parents were expecting of me, I said "yes" to a career suggestion which, I had to admit, sounded a bit more promising than standing at the counter of a bank dressed up to the nines in a Burtons suit.

Matters then proceeded at quite a pace and very soon an interview with Mr Mackenzie was duly organised at few days' notice. I am rather vague as to exactly the sequence of following events but with a degree of relief all round, I found myself with a starting date as a pupil of Mr Mackenzie at John Pritchard and Company at their High Street, Bangor, offices.

The very official-looking legal document which both my parents and Mr Mackenzie became signatures to, bound me to the firm for three years at a cost to my parents, (yes, to my parents), of £300 partly returnable to me as a 'wage' at the rate of £100 per annum for the last of two of the three years of the agreement. Sounds archaic does it not, even for as long ago as the early 60s? Some might even call such an arrangement Dickensian but this sort of legal arrangement was very much the norm in those days, particularly in the legal profession.

And so my career as an auctioneer, or at least as a trainee one, began, and so began the making of arrangements to make the daily journey to Bangor which varied initially between hitching a lift, getting the train and, luxury of all luxuries, an occasional lift with someone my parents knew who worked at the inland revenue office in Bangor.

I should explain at this stage that my parents and I had not signed up for me to train just as an auctioneer. John Pritchard & Company, or JP & Co., as I shall refer to them, were, as well as being old-established auctioneers, prominent in the field of estate agency and surveying and the offices occupied a very prestigious and valuable position right opposite the old town clock in the High Street. Mr Mackenzie, or Mack, as he was referred to locally, had taken over the business after his father Parker Mackenzie, who had, at one time, been prominent as an auctioneer of Welsh Black cattle particularly at the livestock market (or mart) in Menai Bridge, which he ran amongst others in the area.

The office personnel comprised Mack's assistant and experienced right-hand man Derek Goodwin, whose entire career was spent with the Company, Alice Hughes and Mr McCarter who were both on the clerical and financial side of things, and finally the two trainee dogsbodies, yours truly and J Jeremy Jones, a farmer's son from Pwllheli who started in the office with me at precisely the same time. Jeremy subsequently carved himself a very successful career locally as an estate and letting agent in the Llanfairfechan area.

Bangor in the Sixties
We all know that the danger of reminiscing is that usually the rose-tinted spectacles are put on, so that readers, particularly those familiar with the city, will understandably proclaim, "What's he on about, it was never like that, not while I was there, anyway"!

As a university, hospital, cathedral and commercial city, Bangor has possibly not changed dramatically since the early 60s. My apologies to Bangor 2014, but I sincerely believe that, fundamentally, it was a better city in 1960. Yes, it had the university, the hospital and the cathedral. Two of

FORM No. 1.

The Chartered Auctioneers' and Estate Agents' Institute

29, Lincoln's Inn Fields, London, W.C.2

ARTICLES OF CLERKSHIP.

These Articles of Clerkship made the *First* day of *November*. One thousand nine hundred and *Sixty*
Between *Ronald Mackenzie* of *Bank Chambers Bangor*
(hereinafter called "the Principal") a *Fellow* of The Chartered Auctioneers'
and Estate Agents' Institute and a partner in the firm of *John Prichard &*
Bangor of the first part, *Henry Rogers Jones* of
140 Conway Rd Llandudno Junction (hereinafter called "the *Parent") of the
second part and *David Henry Rogers Jones* of
Boderyr Glyn y marl. Rd Llandudno Junction (hereinafter called "the
Pupil") of the third part.

* Note :— If not a Parent alter this word to "Guardian" throughout these Articles

WHEREAS the Pupil is desirous of becoming a member of the Chartered Auctioneers' and Estate Agents' Institute (hereinafter called "the Institute") and has applied to the Principal to accept him as an articled pupil which the Principal has at the request of the Parent agreed to do in a manner hereinafter appearing. NOW THESE PRESENTS WITNESS that in pursuance of the said agreement:

1. IN consideration of the premium of *300* guineas paid by the Parent to the Principal (the receipt whereof the Principal hereby acknowledges) the Principal agrees to take the Pupil as his pupil for the term of *3* years from the *first* day of *November,* One thousand nine hundred and *sixty payable in 3 instalments ∴ 100 gns down and 100 gns each succeeding 1. Nov. 1961 and 1. Nov. 1962.*

2. THE Parent and the Pupil jointly and severally covenant with the Principal as follows:—

(a) That the Pupil of his own free will and with the consent of the Parent binds himself pupil to the Principal for the said term.

(b) That the Pupil will faithfully honestly and diligently serve and obey and perform all the lawful and reasonable commands of the Principal and whomsoever he shall appoint to exercise authority in his office, and in all things conduct and acquit himself as an honest and faithful pupil.

(c) That the Pupil will at all times keep the secrets of the Principal, his Firm and his and their clients, and will not do anything to damage or injure the Principal or his Firm or knowingly suffer the same to be done without acquainting the Principal or some person in authority as aforesaid.

(d) That in case the Pupil shall act contrary to the last preceding covenant, or if the Principal shall sustain or suffer any loss or damage by reason of the misbehaviour neglect or improper conduct of the Pupil, the Parent will make good and reimburse the Principal the amount or value thereof.

Articles of Clerkship details, November 1960

these were, and still are, at the physical heart of the city, but the site of the old C & A Hospital, revered and beloved by so many, is now occupied by, an almost inevitable, supermarket. The old C & A had an aura of its own, with home–grown surgeons, doctors and nursing sisters whose individual names were recognised, and respected, far and wide. The old St David's maternity hospital, the birthplace of so many of the area's population, a short distance down the road, has also disappeared to be replaced by so-called superstores.

The High Street area of the city in the early 60s contained all the major banks, who had proper managers, mostly of great banking experience and whose names were respected and revered throughout the business community. Next door to JP & Co.'s office on one side was the Midland, managed by Mr Thomas, instantly recognised, always in pin-striped suit with furled umbrella and briefcase, all topped by a black trilby hat. On the other side, Lloyds, managed by the equally respected Mr Humphreys. Above our office was Mr R A Coleman, Stockbroker. Yes, in those days, the City of Bangor boasted a stockbroker, again totally revered and respected by all the business community.

Just up the High Street was the Nat.West Bank, distinguished over the years by many good managers but possibly none more so than one Mr Lemuel Jones, affectionately known by everyone as Lem Nat.West. He was famous, amongst other things, for his annual 'Christmas Bash' which his clients and other business contacts almost queued up to be invited to. Lem. was singularly responsible in those days for very many hangovers and resultant days off work!

Fifty years on, in post-breathalyser days, the story of Lem's foray to a banker's function in Llandudno still gets many a room going. The quite prestigious annual dinner had ended with everyone, including Lem, in good spirits until the time came for everyone to make to their vehicles to prepare for the homeward journey. Except that Lem could not find his car. The streets and promenade of Llandudno were scoured with much inebriated assistance from Lem's colleagues but to no avail, until it was decided to report the missing vehicle to the police. Much time was taken up giving all the necessary details until, eventually Lem and his 'assistants' left the police station to make their way home by alternative means which had not yet been decided upon.

As they proceeded down one of Landudno's normally busy side streets, what did they spot parked neatly and proudly, virtually on its own but Lem's shiny limousine. Relief all round as they all piled in for the return journey to Bangor. They had not travelled out of the town's built-up area before the sound of police sirens began to ring in their ears. The Bangor 'charabanc' was pulled up by the roadside only to be pounced upon by several enthusiastic officers who had one thing only in mind – a commendation from their superiors for such a quick and efficient solving of a crime of vehicle theft!

It was never recorded when, exactly, Lem and his colleagues eventually reached Bangor, but it certainly took the police some time to be convinced that this, hitherto highly respected, member of the business community of Bangor was who he said he was, and that the car he was trying to drive back to Bangor was indeed his!

In the 60s, the 'out of town shopping' phenomenon was quite a long way off as far as Bangor was concerned, although the Wellfield shopping centre, just off the main street, would become a reality very soon. The centre of town therefore still had an excellent nucleus of good quality, old – established, family-type businesses such as Robert Roberts, bakers and provision merchants, Williams & Lewis outfitters, Pollecoffs, Jones the Woodworker and many good, well respected butchers' shops, television retailers and the like, and the hub of all this retail activity was the Market Hall, situated right in the middle of the High Street and whose rentals were managed by J P & Co.

The legal profession in Bangor was represented by many highly-respected members of the 'old school', or at least, that's how they appeared to me as a mere nineteen-year-old. There were, to name but a few, Sir Elwyn Jones of Elwyn Jones & Co., Colonel Carter of Carter Vincent & Co., Mr Ioan Y Glynne of Glynne & Co. and Mr Gordon Owen of Owen & Hughes & Co., all of whom were good, and regular, clients of J P & Co.; they were all providers, on a regular basis, of valuable instructions benefitting both the auction side and the estate agency side of the operation.

On the estate agency side, there were not that many companies to choose from in the city. The multiples which gained prominence in the 80s and 90s, had not yet become a feature of the house-selling profession. JP & Co's main rivals were Jones & Beardmore, which was the Bangor branch of a small, old-established group, centred around Abergele, Rhyl and Prestatyn. The Bangor partner was John Lewis and there was not a lot of love lost between him and Mack. The rivalry was accentuated by the fact, that not only was Jones & Beardmore our principal rival on the house-selling side, they were very much our rivals on the auction side too.

Both companies operated the auction side of their businesses in hired Drill Halls – J P & Co. in Menai Bridge and Jones & Beardmore at the Drill Hall in Dean Street, Bangor. (Many years later I was to become very friendly with both John Lewis and his son Jonathan who both became good colleagues and clients.)

Another big asset to Bangor's city centre over so many

years has been the Farrar Road football ground and the sometimes wonderful exploits of Bangor City FC. In the 1960s, the standard of soccer in North Wales was very high indeed. Bangor was not the only standard bearer; Holyhead, Borough United, Flint and Pwllheli were just a few of the other clubs who made names for themselves during what was a golden era for so many participants.

'I was there', as they say, when Bangor City entertained A C Napoli no less, at the Farrar Road ground in the European Cup Winners' cup on 5th September 1962. Whether it was an evening or afternoon fixture I cannot recall, but I was one of 12,000 privileged spectators at the ground on that day to witness the local heroes coming out on top by two goals to nil. They lost the return in Italy by three goals to one and, sadly, the decider at Highbury, Arsenal's famous ground, by two goals to one.

Bangor City lost this time at football, but in terms of putting the city on the map, it had truly won 'hands down'. And just to prove that their exploits were no mere footballing fluke, City took on Cardiff City in the 1964 final of the Welsh Cup beating them at home in the first leg in front of another huge, 8,000 crowd, only to lose the return in Cardiff and the deciding play-off.

As I recall this anecdote at the end of 2013, Bangor City have played their last-ever match at Farrar Road, prior to moving to a new out-of-town ground. The football spectators are now replaced by shoppers as this iconic feature of the city makes way for yet another supermarket.

Proper Pronunciation
Shortly after commencing my articles with Mack, he called me into his office one day and sat me down and after chatting for some while about not much in particular he came out with, what was for me, a bit of a bombshell. "I

think, David that your career as an auctioneer would benefit from a few elocution lessons as it is of vital importance to have clarity and good diction when you're up there on that rostrum."

Elocution lessons? What was the man thinking, was my immediate reaction. Raising my voice a bit and making myself clearly heard on the rostrum surely did not mean going around repeating 'Peter Piper Picked a Peck of Pickled Pepper' or 'How Now, Brown Cow?' And anyway, was this not more the province of little girls rather than aspiring male auctioneers?

Deliberately showing a rather luke-warm reaction to this idea, I prodded my boss for a few more details and a little of the whys and wherefores behind this idea. My enthusiasm scale remained firmly on nought, however, but Mack was the boss, and the boss on this particular issue, had already made his mind up. So elocution lessons it was to be.

Now, coincidentally or what, I don't know, but it transpired that right in my home patch in Llandudno Junction was a lady who gave lessons in elocution. My somewhat suspicious mind immediately started thinking that there was a bit of a conspiracy going on here – between Mack and my mother.

I wondered whether they had already had a chat and that my mother just 'happened to know of a lady elocutionist living down the road'. After all, one cannot imagine many villages, large or small, in North Wales having, of all things, an elocutionist, unless there happened to be a particular demand from one or more, of the private educational establishments in the area. Anyway, theorising and being suspicious were not going to get me anywhere on this issue and so, elocution here we come!

I do not recall my teacher's name, but following the third of four lessons which had been booked with her, and which,

I have to admit, were of quite a constructive nature, she suddenly came out with the suggestion that I "might enjoy amateur dramatics". Now this was becoming a bit ridiculous. Firstly, elocution lessons and now amateur dramatics! Dammit, I only wanted to become an auctioneer. Did all aspiring auctioneers have to go through such rigmarole?

It transpired that my teacher was a keen member of *The Thespians Amateur Dramatic Society* based in Colwyn Bay, which had been operating very successfully in the area since 1946 and had been awarded First Prize on five occasions, at the quite prestigious Colwyn Bay Annual Drama Festival.

Emlyn Williams, Stanley Baker and Richard Burton had always been acting heroes of mine and so, with far more enthusiasm than I had shown for the elocution I said yes, I would like to try my hand at amateur dramatics. The lights of the West End were surely beckoning!

My 'Acting Career' Commences
Whether or not they were desperate for new recruits, I cannot recall, but all I can state is that on the 20th and 21st of October 1961, I appeared in my first production for The Thespians at the Colwyn Theatre. The play, by Jenny Laird and John Fernald, was called '*And No Birds Sing*', in which yours truly played the part of a young Scottish doctor, Kenneth Tweedie.

Jean Ainslie, in her report of the production for the *North Wales Weekly News*, wrote that 'David Rogers Jones showed fire as an irate young doctor.....' It remains quite a coincidence that the Auction House and Business founded by my wife and me in 1992 would be, and indeed still is, situated a couple of doors away from the Colwyn Theatre where my 'acting career' took its first, and only, fledgling steps!

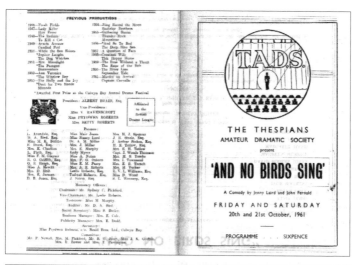

The programme for my debut 'acting career'

Cats in Hirael

I felt pleased and encouraged that after some eighteen months as his pupil, I was beginning to be entrusted by Mack with tasks, both on the property and chattels side, which gave me some leeway and a chance, perhaps to express, and bring to fruition, some of my own ideas. One day I was summoned to his office and instructed to make my way to a house in Hirael (the old sea-port area of the city) to take written details of both the contents and of the property itself.

Hirael is an interesting area, full of smallish terraced properties with rear alleyways, interspersed with the occasional old pub and a corner shop or two, all quite neatly contained in a small area just off the main easterly approach road into the city, with Penrhyn Castle and the old port on the right-hand side.

Mack handed me the key to the property with the warning that I was likely to be challenged by the next-door neighbour, Mr Hughes, who had been entrusted to keep his eye on the property since the death of the elderly lady owner.

I made my way to the rear gate of the little yard of the house via the typical, narrow service lane and just as promised, the 'challenge' from Mr Hughes duly came from a voice on the other side of the adjoining wall between the properties. "Hello, is that Mr Jones from Mr Mackenzie's office", asked the voice, still with no body attached to it.

"Yes it is" I replied, as I tried to locate the elusive Mr Hughes. Suddenly, a cap of the very flat variety appeared just over the coping of the wall, followed by a pair of the rosiest cheeks I'd ever seen on any man. Then followed some scuffling, banging and kicking and I realised that Mr Hughes was putting an orange box in place for him to stand on, in order to check the credentials of the young man on the other side.

Eventually, Mr Hughes declared himself perfectly happy with who I was and proceeded to let me get on with things but with the sudden parting shot, "Good job we got rid of the cats, anyway".

I turned to him immediately, "What do you mean, 'cats' and how many are we talking about?"

"Well, we actually accounted for 19 and found homes for them all, but there could still be a few around as the old lady really was passionate about them".

Then the penny dropped. No wonder my crafty boss had been so keen for me to do a job which, in his words, would be just the task to enhance my experience. Nineteen cats in a two-up, two-down, terraced house, with not an inch of garden was my immediate thought as I prepared, with bated breath and imaginary face mask, to enter the property. I turned the key in the lock, watched by Mr Hughes and opened the door, whereupon I was assaulted by the most horrendous smell I had ever experienced. Not only was it foul but there were cats' toilets everywhere and it really was as much as I could do to avoid being physically sick on the spot. The occupier had passed away at least six weeks previously so the scenario is quite easy to imagine.

As quickly as I possibly could, and without touching anything, I took measurements of all the rooms and made notes of all important details, before making the decision to report back to Mack that the contents of the property were of no value whatsoever and a complete write-off, due to having been contaminated beyond economical restoration by the smell of so many cats in such a relatively confined area.

I made my exit and returned to the office to report back to the boss with my findings and recommendations. These were, basically, to remove all the contents forthwith to the nearest disposal tip (uncontaminated, they would all have had good potential value) and arrange for the house to be fumigated as urgently as possible.

Mack expressed some degree of surprise at my recommendations but readily embraced them, with the comment that I had "done a good job". I strongly suspect to this day that my boss knew full well of the state of the property in Hirael and that by sending me there, he was firstly avoiding the task himself, which was the prerogative of a boss and that, secondly, it was some form of test as to how his young pupil might handle the task.

In over fifty years, I cannot recall anything which has been invented to cure and restore, soft furnishings and the like which have been contaminated by cigarette and cigar smoke and the smells formed by the prolonged occupation of a property by animals such as dogs and cats.

The inventor of such a product would surely make a fortune!

Sand at Rhosneigr

It had been a relatively quiet period towards late Spring 1961, nothing dramatic in the offing except for the regular routine of the furniture auctions at the Drill Hall in Menai Bridge.

Mack breezed into the office one morning. "I have an assignment for you, David". I was intrigued by the word 'assignment' as opposed perhaps, to the simpler word 'task'.

"We're going to Rhosneigr tomorrow, crack of dawn, and I'll explain to you on the way what it is that I want doing. Bring with you light shoes and clothing, some food and drink and, most importantly, don't forget to bring with you the 100-foot measuring tape."

The shoes, clothing and food sounded quite promising, particularly as the destination was to be the popular and up-market seaside village on Anglesey's north-west coast. But the 100-foot tape mystified me.

The journey the following day along the old A5 highway from Bangor was pleasant and uneventful but I quickly had to divert from the pleasantries of the scenery in order to concentrate on the finer details of the 'assignment' which Mack had prepared for me.

It transpired that a long-established client of the company was the owner of considerable tracts of land in and around, the Rhosneigr area. Nice and popular though Rhosneigr clearly is, in many people's eyes it has always felt to be somewhat blighted by its close proximity to the airfield at RAF Valley, a strategic aircrew training establishment with one of its runways terminating quite close to the village itself. The constant noise of the aircraft doing take-offs and touch landings can be quite disconcerting, but no doubt the locals will say that they are quite used to the noise and that they are more than happy to tolerate it as long as the airfield continues to give much-needed employment to the area.

The Property Services Agency,(the PSA), who were at the time, the agents for the military in its various forms, wished to acquire from Mack's client an area of land in order to extend the airfield runway which, in those days terminated some distance away from the Rhosneigr Golf Course.

The actual surface area of the land which the PSA wished to acquire was more or less pre-determined from Ordnance Survey maps. It was simply a matter of agreeing a price for the acreage involved. The more complicated part, I was soon to be informed, was the sand. I turned slightly incredulously to look at my boss, who, by his own reaction, was evidently expecting some sort of surprised reaction from this pupil whom he had chosen to carry out the assignment.

"Sand, how do you mean sand?" I asked somewhat disbelievingly. Apparently, the client had, to his credit, been doing his homework and had discovered that dune sand, of which there were substantial hillocks all around, commanded something of a premium price due to the property building boom which, at that time, was beginning to take off. All that it required to turn into top-class, valuable building material was to put it through a proper industrial filtering and washing process.

The client, to his credit, had realized that the sand on his land was of far greater value than the land itself. The penny suddenly dropped and I knew what was coming.

"Your task, young man, is to work out for me the volume of sand lying on the area of land which is the subject of the forthcoming sale to the PSA. You've more or less got the whole day to complete the task, I've got other things to do and clients to see in and around Rhosneigr and I'll call at the end of the afternoon to pick you up. I think that you've got all you need, take your time and you can let me have your calculations in the office by the end of play tomorrow." And then he was gone.

I waited for Mack to get into his Morris 1800 car (a veritable limousine in its time) and depart down the track towards the main road leaving a cloud of the yellow stuff in his wake. I chuckled to myself at his reference to my having 'all I needed' to carry out what was clearly going to be a monumental task – a 100-foot measuring tape and some water and sandwiches!

I sat down to survey my surrounds and began immediately to have horrible thoughts. I was about half-way through my pupilage as a trainee auctioneer. If I failed this assignment, was that the end of any aspirations I had of becoming an auctioneer? Would it mean, after all, my ending up in the bank with the boring hours which that would entail?

I needed a plan and I needed one very quickly, as the prospect of sitting in the spring sunshine staring at mounds of sand appealed very little to me. I suddenly recalled that somewhere back at home in some old school mathematics books was a formula for calculating the cubic volume of a solid contained in a square, a rectangle or, hopefully, a triangle.

My Heath Robinson-type plan was to measure roughly (very roughly!) one of the large mounds of sand (of which there were approximately nine dotted around the client's land) and to adopt that particular mound as the average of the whole lot. Very scientific indeed! I felt that if Heath Robinson could do it, so could I.

The 100-foot tape was about to earn its living, or, more importantly, to rescue me from the sack! I took stock of my surroundings, got up, dusted myself down and made a conscious effort to look 'official'. I was rather anxious to ensure that, unknown to me, I was not being watched by the local 'bush telegraph' who would doubtless take more than a little delight in reporting 'odd goings-on' in the dunes down by the golf club! It took me about twenty-five minutes to clamber up my 'average' dune, measure its length along the base and then its approximate height.

I decided to have my sandwiches and water and to go for a wander and to get back in plenty of time to resume looking suitably industrious for when the boss returned to take me back to Bangor. I began to dread the probability of being quizzed by him as to how I had approached the practicalities of the day's assignment.

The journey was quiet, uneventful and without the awkward questions which I was dreading. Nevertheless, I had definitely come to the conclusion that I had, with little doubt, performed my last task as a trainee auctioneer. I just could not conceive that my amateurish, pie-in-the-sky calculations, on which an important land sale transaction depended, were going to be acceptable to the parties involved.

I went home that evening to dig out the maths books but

fully resigned to the fate which was to befall me the following day. I decided that all I could do was to at least produce some half-credible calculations which might, just might, give a slight impression of an effort of some sorts having been made.

I arrived at the office the following morning and decided to put myself out of my misery by presenting my calculation to Mack as soon as was practical. I knocked on his door, walked in and presented to him neatly on paper my calculation of the total tonnage of sand involved in the transaction between his client and the PSA acting on behalf of the RAF.

234,241 tons of sand was the calculation or, rather, the totally unscientific guess which I had decided to present him with. He took it and thanked me and proceeded to chat casually about another matter in hand. I left his office and wondered whether I should proceed immediately to gather the few effects I had, in readiness for what I assumed was to be my imminent departure.

Nothing further happened that day but on the following day, sharp at nine o'clock, the summons came to go to Mack's office, by which time I was very much resigned to the fate about to befall me.

"David, I just want to thank you for all your hard work in Rhosneigr the other day. Your calculations were very impressive, so much so that the PSA is very likely, without question, to accept without challenge the figures as submitted as the Ministry is very anxious to proceed to acquire our client's land with the very minimum of delay."

Talk about throwing sand in people's eyes!

The Drill Hall
John Pritchard and Company and Jones and Beardmore were the main, regular auction operators in the Bangor area

in the 1960s. Both deadly rivals, it could be said, with each vying to get local goods into their respective auction venues – my firm John Pritchard operating out of the hired drill hall in Menai Bridge and Beardmores, as they were locally referred to – operating out of Bangor's drill hall in Dean Street.

If a man could be said to have the bearing and presence of an auctioneer, then that person would surely be Ronald McKenzie – Mack. He was a man of powerful stature, tall and proportionately wide, hair swept back and handsome with a powerful auctioneer's voice to match.

Auctions in those days had none of the sophisticated, computer-led procedures which are the norm today. Sale lists, sale sheets, bills to the buyers and statements to the sellers would all have been hand-written. But one thing which neither time nor fancy inventions have been able to alter, is that one vital ingredient for the success of any auction – a good auctioneer. And Mack was just that.

He positively commanded the auction whether he was selling low-grade items, high-value antiques or residential or agricultural property. He had that one vital requirement of an accomplished auctioneer at the top of his profession – that ability to give as enthusiastic and as convincing a sales pitch when offering for sale a piece of dross as when offering something of far greater importance and value.

His father Mr Parker McKenzie before him, ran the livestock market specializing in Welsh Black cattle at Menai Bridge, so the grounding was there and Mack would have been taught by an auctioneer-father who had experienced the really hard times in the fortunes of the island's agricultural industry.

The Drill Hall auctions in Menai Bridge were held on a fairly regular basis and the success and smooth running of the system was helped by the fact that, almost next door, was the yard and HQ of a well-known and long-established family firm of furniture removers, Tom Jones & Company.

They were used on a regular basis by Mack whenever clients required their goods collecting for delivery to the auction. There was a handy arrangement in reverse also. Purchasers of goods at the auction would often require their items to be delivered home and so there existed an unofficial arrangement whereby two of Tom Jones' men would act as porters in the Drill Hall for the duration of the auction, the clear advantage to them being that by knowing that certain sold items were destined for Tom Jones' customers, they could be stored after sale in a particular location which avoided double-handling on their part. Crafty people these furniture removers!

Two other porters in the Drill Hall – yours truly and my colleague Jeremy Jones were there supposedly to learn the task of being auctioneers, in the course of which we also had to carry out our fair share, (sometimes more than our fair share) of moving heavy sideboards, wardrobes and the like from their stored position in the hall to the front for all the seated prospective customers to cast a final glance before placing a bid. Fifty years on, many auction houses now display on a screen, each pre-photographed lot as it comes up for sale, thus rendering the saleroom porter's life a somewhat easier one!

I suppose that values and the prices of goods in a saleroom are always going to be the preoccupation of an auctioneer, as they still are very much with me. I well remember some of the prices prevailing at our auctions between 1960 and 1962.

Welsh oak dressers, press cupboards, grandfather clocks and the like were just not in vogue and were extremely cheap. Grandfather clocks, or, to use the correct name, long case clocks, in the Drill Hall auctions were a fairly standard, regular price – £5 and Welsh dressers between £10 and £15. I clearly recall one auction where a long-case clock doubled its usual price to make an 'astronomical' £9 and within an hour of the end of the auction, the rumour had gone round Menai Bridge like wildfire that Mack had sold 'one of those grandfather clocks for £9 – what was the blooming world coming to?'

During this period, one of the local antique dealers and regular Drill Hall attenders was Alf Goddard, a Bangor-based member of a very well-known family of North Wales antique dealers. He and his band of fellow dealers were, at the time, very welcome customers at all the local auctions as they appeared to be the only ones showing the slightest bit of interest in Welsh oak and other traditional furniture. Alf Goddard was a lovely, polite, old-fashioned type of gent. Small, always immaculately suited with waistcoat and regulation flat cap and, without fail, the shiniest pair of boots one could ever imagine.

His mode of transport when doing his rounds was a Morris Minor pick-up which was always easily recognizable by two things – Alf's flat cap, not his face, just about visible over the steering wheel of the Morris and, if it had been a particularly fruitful day on his rounds, as many as three welsh dressers in the pick-up – two in the back and the third on top of them with the rack of the dresser overhanging the driver's cab!

As Welsh dressers and other oak furniture eventually made a recovery in popularity and demand, many were the occasions when I heard this lament of an Anglesey farmer or family member: *'Dwi'n cofio'n nhad yn rhoi'r fwyall i hen ddresel y teulu – 'roedd o werth mwy fel coed tan'* (I remember my father giving the family dresser the chop as it was worth more as firewood).

Social changes and tastes are interesting – it is so easy to forget that the Welsh dresser that we know and so revere today, started life off as a cupboard in the kitchen for storing food. Later generations have elevated the status of the dresser to that of a 'show piece' now given pride of place in one of the better rooms of the house.

Mack's initiation or blooding of a pupil at the Drill Hall was a scary affair for one principal reason. His regular customers who had been attending his auctions for many years had a pretty fair idea when each of his pupil's time was up. They could calculate how long a certain person had been doing the 'donkey work' and as they were pretty familiar with the training time-span given to each of his pupils, the regulars would have a fair idea when a person's inauguration was about due.

A few weeks before the dreaded time, old regulars at the Drill Hall would ask veiled questions such as "how long have you been with Mack now, David? Still enjoying it are you? I suppose you're looking forward sometime to getting up there and showing us all what you can do?" And so it went on.

And then, 'bang,' it happened, some twenty-five minutes into a particularly well-attended auction Mack stopped abruptly, the whole place went even quieter than normal and he delivered a brief introductory few words – "Now you're all pretty familiar with David here, who's been with us for over a year, he's taking my seat today for a few lots so help him all you can by keeping as quiet as possible and making your bids clear and with more deliberation than usual."

"There we are young man, it's all yours, don't forget to scan front to back and side to side for all bids, and don't worry about speed, that'll come later."

And that was it, up I went onto the rostrum for the first time in my life, not with too much disgrace, I recall, as a few of the hardened regulars came up to me at the end with some encouraging back-slapping.

After sand dunes at Rhosneigr and the certainty, or so I feared, of the sack, things were beginning to look up!

Fakes, Forgeries and Tourist Trash!
I felt that I was continuing to make reasonable progress on the rostrum during our monthly auctions at the Drill Hall in Menai Bridge. I think that Jeremy Jones had already decided that the rostrum side of the operation was not really his scene. Mack continued to display his utter mastery of the rostrum and did not suffer fools gladly whilst occupying the chair.

During a long auction he would usually hand over proceedings to Derek for him to continue and I would be given a session which tended to increase in length with every auction. From very small beginnings of fifteen lots or so, I was now handling between fifty and one hundred lots depending on the size of a particular auction.

If the boss had a comment or criticism to make whilst I was selling, he would express it there and then, in full view and in sight of, all the customers. Any embarrassment caused was well intended – hopefully you would not repeat whatever error it was that Mack was criticising you for in the first place.

I well remember an occasion when my confidence was fairly sky-high and I was rattling along with some lots at a fair old pace. Suddenly, whilst in full flight, a shout in my direction from Mack. Everyone froze, waiting for the blast. "David, this is not a Grand Prix race, slow down just a little bit, but not by too much as all these people sitting in front of you are not exactly snails either!"

The 'antique trade' in the 60s was a relatively uncomplicated circus compared with the late 70s, 80s and all the way up to the present 21st century. Anything described as an 'antique' was usually just that, one hundred years old or over, no more, no less, no argument. Our recovery from the war was just over and the population was beginning to wonder how to enjoy itself.

Package holidays were the forerunners of things to come. Our very first 'cheap holiday' I remember well: ten days in Opatjia, Yugoslavia, flying Britannia Airways from Luton Airport, for a very modest-sounding £45 each! On this momentous holiday, my wife Margaret sampled a concoction described on the hotel menu as 'calf's lung soup.' She hasn't sampled any again but has milked the occasion as a talking point on several occasions since!

But what on earth have package holidays got to do with the antique trade in the 1960s you may ask? Actually, quite a great deal. With their increasing popularity came the tendency for all of us to support, unwittingly, industries on the other side of the water, geared, very efficiently, to the manufacture of countless numbers of touristy trinkets which were brought home as gifts to granny and other members of the family as mementoes of a wonderful holiday.

Unfortunately, it did not take granny very long to start believing that after a few years proudly displayed in the china cabinet in the parlour, the ornaments had begun to increase in value; after all, 'they were twenty years old', or whatever. The whole scenario of the tourist trinket has continued to this very day with poor people believing that the glazed plaster figurine of a little girl with a basket of flowers, brought over all the way from Italy or Spain by a loving niece, was bound, a few years later, to have increased in value. Nothing could be further from reality. There's a cruel saying in the business even to this day – 'tourist trash doesn't change its spots!'

Another area of little, or no, concern in the 60s was the

sale of ivory tusks and ornaments. So many items had come over with returning colonials, explorers and service personnel that even in today's heavily-regulated environment, those items, with proper documentation and provenance, are able to be disposed of quite legitimately. But compared with so many things today, where form-filling, signed in quadruple, is the frustrating norm, the 60s were a relatively free and easy environment for the auctioneer and dealers alike.

I feel thankful that, as a student auctioneer in the 60s, with all I had to learn and absorb, a field I did not have to concern myself with, simply because there weren't any – was that of fakes and copies, at the lower end of the market. To be quite clear, there is a very important difference between a fake and a legitimate copy. In simple terms, a fake is an object which has been made to deliberately mislead and to give a buyer or owner the mistaken belief that the item is genuine and of the original age that the object should be. Provided that a copy of an item is stated to be just that, there is no problem. A print of a painting is, after all, just that – a legitimate copy prepared by a particular printing process, and, as we all know, prints, etchings, engravings and the like form an important collecting field in their own right.

China, is one of many countries in the Far East whose enterprise and burgeoning manufacturing power has been responsible, during the last quarter of the twentieth century, for the huge proliferation in the appearance in the United Kingdom of fake goods of an almost unbelievable choice and range.

Designer clothes, luggage and handbags, perfumes, watches, jewellery and other items are very much the norm, but seldom concern auctioneers and those in the trade. Add to that brief list Lalique glassware, Clarice Cliff pottery, 'Art Deco' figurines, Titanic 'memorabilia' and 'signed' sporting goods and clothing, and you then have an idea just what a potential problem everyone in our business now has. It is important also not to place all the blame on our oriental brethren as our very own UK has its fair share of chancers and opportunists!

Whilst problems such as these were not our concern in sleepy North Wales in the early 60s, we, along with other auctioneers, did have one fairly major issue to contend with on a regular basis – the 'ring.' For the uninitiated, a rather complex-sounding explanation of this phenomenon might be deemed worthwhile. In very basic terms, the 'ring' could be described as a conspiracy by one or more potential purchasers (usually dealers) at an auction, to deprive the seller (the vendor) of the full and proper value of an item simply by all members, except one, of the ring agreeing not to bid on an item for sale. In other words, they were agreeing beforehand, not to bid against one another.

The interesting part comes at the end of the auction! The offending group would then disappear, maybe to a vehicle or local café, to conduct its own 'auction'. So, if the item at the legitimate auction has, let's say, made £100 when its true worth was £200, the 'ring' has benefited to the tune of £100.

Simple arithmetic, you may say. If there are five persons involved in the conspiracy on this particular day, one of the party will be the successful bidder at whatever higher figure it has been knocked down for in the ensuing illegal 'auction'. Should that figure be £200, the winner then pays his four fellow conspirators the difference between the two prices, which is shared equally by the four remaining participants. In simple terms, four of the five in the scam will receive £25 each for doing precisely nothing. Multiply this by several lots, some at considerably higher prices, and the extent of such activity can be appreciated.

The policing of the 'ring's' activities at that time proved

to be extremely difficult, although I do recall that some thirty years ago, one North Wales dealer was caught in, what one might call, a ring sting, and was duly hauled up and fined. But that occasion was a rare thing, for the simple reason that the so-called 'crime' of being in a 'ring' was exceedingly hard to police and to prove in a court of law.

The 'ring' today is more or less a thing of the past, but it has been interesting over the years listening not only to people expounding the merits of the Act relating to the ring, but also to those very interesting opinions criticising the Act for being so dated and barely able to handle the realities of modern-day auctioneering.

I have heard so many opinions on this issue over the years that I myself, have ended up 'on the fence' over it. And I'm the auctioneer! "The 'ring,' in the saleroom is better, on a bad day, than no ring at all", I have heard said. Then a good auctioneer, familiar with the true value of an item, should be able to raise the price himself, against the ring, thus ensuring a reasonably fair price for his client.

Then the most telling question of all. "What's the difference between the 'ring' and two ladies who walk into a saleroom after a bout of fashion shopping?" One spots an item they both really like, but each agrees that one of them likes the item just slightly more than the other. So they determine that one of them will bid on the lot, thus ensuring that they are not bidding against one another. Is that supposed to be a conspiracy? Yes, but a very mild one, surely, perpetrated by two nice ladies but with the same end result!

Today's technology, coupled with the general scarcity of rare and quality items, more or less ensures that the competition in the saleroom eliminates the perceived detrimental effect of the 'ring'. But I have to state that in the early sixties when antiques were going cheap, there were very many occasions in the Drill Hall in Menai Bridge when

Mack was grateful on a sale day to see the 'ring' turn up!

Harry Parry

As well as the assistance of Tom Jones' men as unofficial porters in the Drill Hall, we also had Harry Parry. (I think that we, the Welsh are the only ones in the world who can boast having up to four versions of the same Christian and surname – hence Harry Parry (1), Harry Parri (2), Harri Parri (3) and Harri Parry (4).

Harry Parry (no.1 version) lived on the Tyddyn To estate in Menai Bridge and he and Mack were well known to one another. Harry was a lovable, roguish character who 'knew his way around,' and was familiar with many of the local watering holes. In today's jargon, Harry would be known as a 'multi-tasker.' As well as helping in the Drill Hall on sale days, he carried out odd gardening and other jobs locally and, quite importantly, he was most useful as a general sorter at properties whose contents we had been instructed to tidy prior to their removal to the Drill Hall.

Now Harry had this peculiar trait, some might say commendable, depending on their point of view. He was very much against (for this, read – 'totally opposed' or 'did not recognize') Her Majesty's Inspector of Taxes. Indeed, whenever anything 'official' landed through Harry's letterbox, he simply wrote on the unopened envelope 'Deceased' and promptly popped it back into the nearest post box! Quite simply, Harry was a 'cash man' who really was most reluctant to share his hard-earned wages with the government when it could so much more easily and enjoyably be spent at the Liverpool Arms in the Village!

On one memorable occasion Jeremy Jones, my fellow pupil and I, had been delegated to visit a house near Llandegfan to prepare and tidy, prior to Tom Jones and Co. moving in to remove the entire contents to the Drill Hall just down the road. Harry was also with us busying himself sorting out the kitchen contents, when he must suddenly have spotted the two very smartly dressed gentlemen walking up the path of the house towards the front door.

Before a finger had even been placed on the door bell, Harry had disappeared via the back door as if by magic; not a good-bye, not an explanation, nothing, leaving JJ and me staring at one another in utter disbelief. Both of us swallowed hard in an effort to regain reasonable composure prior to facing our very official-looking visitors.

One of us opened the door, to be politely greeted by "Good morning, sir, we were just wondering how the Lord Jesus comes into your everyday life and whether we can ask if you're interested in joining our flock."

Religious campaigners, not tax inspectors! A happy ending, but one which did not prevent Harry from being completely out of contact and 'absent without leave' until at least three days later!

Uncle Goes Missing

The following scenario is one that auctioneers have still to deal with on a regular basis. Whilst technology has come to benefit most aspects of our daily lives, there is very little it can do to alleviate, or hurry up the processes after the death of a relative or loved one.

There is always so much for families and executors to do that it is so easy to understand the almost apologetic way in which they find themselves having to carry out tasks they've never experienced before. So many express guilt at having to rummage through the personal effects of someone they might have been chatting to the previous week. But, if it is of any consolation to them, the work of locating and identifying property deeds and other financial documents is part of a very necessary process.

Late afternoon one Thursday when we were all making

plans to go home after a reasonably productive day, Derek took a phone call from a gentleman in Birmingham seeking the urgent services of the company. An aged uncle living in Llanfairfechan had passed away that week and there was a fairly urgent need to empty the tenanted premises as soon as practicable having regard for the funeral, and other essential arrangements which were going to have to be made. The added difficulty was that the nephew was due to fly back the following week to his workplace in the Middle East.

Some families do not have time constraints and can therefore ease themselves in to what is going to be a difficult process, unlike this new client from Birmingham, who did not have time on his side. It was immediately agreed that we would visit the property early the following day. Much work and telephoning was likely to be required bearing in mind the looming week-end, and so it proved.

The contents, which included a few quite saleable antiques, were not going to present a problem in themselves, just the urgency to get them out of the property within a very narrow timescale so that the nephew could leave the country with reasonable peace of mind.

The programme was quite straightforward. Funeral the following Tuesday, removers arranged by us, to clear the property on the Wednesday, with the nephew returning to the Middle East on the Thursday. Our instructions were clear; we were to empty the property of its contents in its entirety.

Not only did everything work out satisfactorily in the eyes of the client – he seemed to be more than satisfied with the service he'd been given at such short notice – we happened to have sufficient space in the Drill Hall for an auction due to take place the following week for us to be able to drop them off in Menai Bridge without the need for costly double-handling and storage.

The day of the auction loomed and, as usual, the viewing took place during the afternoon of the previous day. Late that afternoon, Derek took a phone call asking him to telephone, very urgently, a number in the Middle East. As we had no other clients there at that time, Derek guessed who the caller was, but was puzzled and slightly worried about the possible reason for the call.

The connection made, Derek prepared himself for the usual pre-chat niceties but before he had a chance, out came the agitated pleadings of the nephew on the other end of the line. "Mr Goodwin, thank God I've managed to get hold of you, I've completely forgotten uncle and I remembered you'd told me that the auction was being held tomorrow."

"I'm sorry," replied Derek, "I don't really understand what the problem is. You say that you've forgotten uncle, whose cremation, I recall, took place in Bangor last week."

"That's the very point" came the reply. "After the cremation, I brought uncle's ashes with me back to Llanfairfechan and left them in a small casket in a prominent place in the parlour for me to take them with me on Thursday. But with all that I had to do and remember, I completely forgot to remove uncle, as I'd intended. Please tell me that you've got him there safely in Menai Bridge."

Rather mischievously, I recall, Derek, with the slightest hint of a grin on his face, pronounced that he would send out a search party immediately into the darkest corners of the Drill Hall to seek out the casket containing uncle and he would telephone the nephew back, hopefully with the good news he was praying for, as urgently as possible

A happy ending to the story is that uncle was duly found lurking in a box in the Drill Hall, from which he exited without the slightest murmur or hint of resistance!

Technology, 1960's

Bearing in mind that the computers and laptops, mobile telephones, photocopiers and other technological paraphernalia now commonplace in our twenty first century, had barely been thought of in the 1960s, I just wonder sometimes how we all managed in the running of a pretty successful estate agency and auctioneering business at that time.

Firstly, telephones. These were of the black Bakelite GPO, heavy-as-a sack-of potatoes type which nowadays are something of a collector's item. I seem to recall that one of the upstairs offices, possibly Mack's, had an extension but the exact operation of this escapes me. At least when you dialled, you had to engage your fingers in the different holes of the dial and, unlike today's mobiles with their tiny, barely-raised buttons, it was really quite difficult to mis-dial.

Telephones in those days had an innocent simplicity about them. My 'Nain' on my mother's side was born and bred in Criccieth, that lovely jewel on the Cambrian Coast. Up until the late 50s or even early 60s, Criccieth had its own manned (or in Criccieth's case, womanned) telephone exchange.

If you wanted a Criccieth number, you dialled the exchange, gave the number required to the operator and she would put you through

My mother, as a dutiful daughter, would ring up on a fairly regular basis to have a bit of a chat and to check on Nain's health and on the local gossip etc. I recall one instance when mother rang the operator and gave Nain's number only to be told that "Mrs Griffiths (Nain) had gone shopping that morning to Pwllheli on the bus with her friend Mrs Price and wouldn't be back until early afternoon"! Talk about gossip-mongering and early telephone hacking, Criccieth style!

Back to the office. The 1960s version of a computer or

laptop was the plain and simple typewriter. It required little or no servicing, apart from a change of ribbon and an occasional dusting with a blow brush, and there were no outside charges to pay. All the office work, including the all-important property sales particulars, was typed out on a trusty Remington. A sheet of carbon paper was the accepted means of making a copy and errors were often obliterated by 'Tippex,' a gooey, white concoction which dried quite quickly on application.

But the *piece de resistance* of the whole tiny array of technology in that office was the Gestetner.

This monster was the forerunner of the photocopier, a brute of a thing which looked like a cross between a tombola drum and something out of a metal-worker's shed. Sale particulars were firstly typed out on a thickish paper screen, notched down both sides. The choice of printing fonts was nil and there was no such thing as being able to include a photograph, even of the simplest variety, of the property being offered for sale.

On completion of the typing of the screen, (one side only, incidentally), it was notched onto the pre-inked, Gestetner drum, the copy paper loaded and the drum turned with the side handle until the desired number of copies had been run off. Whilst this might sound easy so far, the real skill lay in the inking of the drum which was a totally manual task. It was one invariably left to the experienced Alice Hughes, simply because the slightest error in over-inking could, (and indeed, had been known to) render the operator looking like someone who had just completed a long shift down a very deep coal mine.

Not long afterwards saw a huge (!) advance in the improvement of property sales particulars, the 'Mini-Print'. Someone came along with the idea of taking a photograph of a property on sale, in our case with our trusty 35 mm.

'instant' film camera.

The film was sent to a new-style photographic laboratory and within a few days, a batch of tiny prints, little more than postage stamp size, would arrive in the office, all with adhesive backs, to be manually and individually stuck onto each of the sale particulars in the space left by the typist somewhere near the title of the property. Progress indeed!

Further progress in this technologically unexciting era, saw the introduction of the electric typewriter followed by the 'personal word processor,' a sort of new-fangled typewriter with an added small screen above the keyboard.

For the preparation of sale particulars, rooms were measured with a long, cloth tape measure, often encased in leather with a brass winding handle. Today's measurements are taken with a nice small, hand-held electronic device which emits a beam from wall to wall and gives off an accurate reading to the operator.

Land areas were quoted in acres, not hectares as today and every acre had 4840 honest square yards contained in it. Area, weight and volume measurements in this era were, thankfully, quoted in good, old-fashioned yards and feet, and pounds and ounces etc.

I should like to think that my enduring fondness for a little, 'good old-fashioned' mental arithmetic stems from those days in Bangor when arithmetic just had to be of the mental variety as, even then, the introduction of the pocket calculator was still some way off as an alternative.

The nearest thing to a mechanical calculator was located in Mr McCarter's accounts office. This was in the form of a heavy block of metal containing an array of buttons, which the operator pressed and then pulled down on the handle located down the side of the machine. A paper roll had to be attached to a spool and this gave a print-out of the button-pusher's efforts.

I recall that the proper name for this was 'adding machine', an un-exciting description if ever there was one! 'Pocket calculator' does, even today, sound a little better.

(Un) Crowded Auction at Caernarfon

Sometime in early 1961, J P & Co. was instructed by the Glynllifon Estate to offer by auction a smallholding near Caernarfon, which it had deemed surplus to its requirements. The estate used the company as its independent auctioneers, despite having an estate office and manager whose work mainly concentrated on the estate's vast acreage and all the tenants and the problems associated with them.

Mack would be the auctioneer, and the solicitor acting for the Estate the experienced and impressive Ieuan ap Gwilym Hughes (affectionately and widely known as Yappy), the partner at the Caernarfon office of the old-established law firm, Carter Vincent and Company.

Mere mention of Yappy's name routinely in conversation would not go anywhere near to describing the real character that he was. To spot Yappy in one of the town's streets or near his favourite haunt, the quay, you would be looking for a weather-beaten, Pickwickian face with rimless glasses perched nose-end, an open-necked shirt and open-tread sandals often found poring over legal papers in his open-topped car down on Castle Quay.

Indeed, I recall once being told that Yappy used to see more clients on the Quay than in his actual office! He was, you understand, very much a sea-loving man and I well remember later on in my career visiting him in his office to deliver some papers. I really thought that I was entering a cross between a ship's chandlery and a scene from one of Dickens' novels. There were the usual ranks of legal volumes along the walls, Yappy's massive, paper-strewn desk in the middle, and then, quite incongruously, all manner of boat gear ranging from coiled ropes, a couple of small coloured buoys, some odd bits of netting and even a small yacht anchor!

Welcome to the offices of Ieuan ap Gwilym Hughes, solicitor of this parish. None of these delightful eccentricities, however, detracted one iota from his professionalism and popularity as a solicitor of the highest calibre.

Back to the auction, or not quite. Despite the widespread and long-established use of the auction system as a means of selling, not only property, but any other conceivable object under the sun, and despite the knowledge members of the public now have concerning auctions in general, due to television and 'the' media, there still exists a certain mystique with regard to some aspects of the system.

It may not be widely known that in auction law, an auctioneer represents his client, the seller, as his agent and, as such he, the auctioneer is allowed to 'bid' on the seller's (the vendor's) behalf in order to raise the price to the minimum figure, known as the Reserve Price, which the seller may have set. Thus, if at an auction, only one bidder commences the bidding on an item, in order to raise the figure to the required minimum price, the auctioneer will bid against the bidder on his client's behalf.

The skill of the auctioneer in such a situation is to make it look, and sound, in a natural and credible way that the saleroom is, in fact, full of keen, voluble bidders when, in fact, exactly the opposite may be the case.

The venue for the sale by auction of the Llandwrog smallholding was the Royal Hotel in Caernarfon, a frequent venue for this type of event. As is customary, a room had been set aside with rows of comfortable chairs for potential buyers and a top table for the auctioneer and solicitor. It was not unusual for potential buyers and the merely curious, particularly in the case of an agricultural property, to gather at the bar of the hotel for a quick snifter before proceedings began or, in the case of a serious bidder, to boost oneself with a bit of pre-auction 'Dutch Courage.'

The bar area, some twenty minutes or so prior to the auction time, would always be a good indicator as to the likely size of the day's crowd. I had taken it upon myself at the twenty-minute mark to pop my head around the nearby bar door to count up the number of imbibing farmer customers. Result – not one! With only five minutes to go, I was despatched by Mack to the bar area and to report back the numbers gathered. There was no one there!

I returned to the auction room and viewed somewhat glumly, and rather alarmingly, the thirty or so, empty chairs. Except for one.

Seated contentedly right in the front row, having almost crept in unseen, was a farmer. I could tell he was a farmer from the way he was clothed including a pair of boots which looked as if they'd just traipsed through some very muddy fields.

Two minutes to go and just the four of us in a room which had suddenly began to look cavernous to say the least – Mack the auctioneer, Yappy Hughes, the solicitor, yours truly the junior dogsbody and – one farmer.

On the stroke of three o'clock, Mack rose to his feet with "Good Afternoon." He would normally have said "Ladies and Gentlemen," but as there were none of the former and only one of the latter, nothing more than good afternoon would have been relevant. "It's a pleasure for us as a company to be offering you today on behalf of the Glynllifon Estate, this most attractive smallholding of eighteen acres, on a Freehold basis and with unencumbered vacant possession."

"Before I invite bids, I should like to ask my friend and colleague Mr Ap Hughes of Carter Vincent and Company Caernarfon, acting on behalf of the Estate, to read out the conditions of sale and to invite any questions arising from those conditions."

Yappy rose to his feet, spectacles right at the end of his rosy red nose, suit with tie, the latter knotted in a manner suggestive of someone unused to wearing one, and Yappy's trademark sandals with no socks. Now any observer in that auction room with his or her eyes closed, listening to these two professionals, Mack and Yappy, doing what came perfectly natural to them, would have been absolutely convinced that they were speaking to a roomful of people, such was the smoothness and authority of their delivery.

Just as Yappy was completing his reading of the sale conditions, I looked towards the solitary farmer and noticed with some consternation that he had a facial twitch, a sort of involuntary jerk of his chin every thirty seconds or so, but as it seemed to have a fairly regular pattern and frequency to it, I gave it little further thought.

Yappy sat down, there being no questions raised concerning the legal conditions and handed over to Mack who, without further ado, invited opening bids for the smallholding with the usual reminder that "upon the fall of the hammer, the purchaser would be required to sign a binding contract and to pay a 10 per cent deposit there and then."

Despite Mack's superbly convincing rhetoric, my gaze remained embarrassingly fixed to the floor as the 'charade' continued with his invitation for an opening bid of £3,500, then £3,000, then £2,500 and then I heard the magic words, "thank you, I have an opening bid of £2,000… £2,200… £2,400… £2,600" at which point I decided to look up, just in time to see the farmer performing one of his involuntary twitches.

"£2,900 I now have," continued Mack by now in full flow. "It's against you, sir, in the front row," then another twitch – "£3,000 from you, sir," at which point there were no further 'bids' forthcoming.

"The bidding now stands at £3,000 with you, sir, at the front row, and the hammer is up for the final time. All finished? All done?" asked Mack for the final time, as if there were fifty people in the room. Down came the hammer in dramatic fashion with an echoing and victorious crack on the table:

"Yours sir, there in the front row for £3,000. Congratulations."

This was the point at which I was absolutely convinced that our farmer would get up, apologise most profusely and explain that due to a facial twitch which he had had since his teens, he was not, in fact bidding and indeed had not the slightest interest in the purchase of an eighteen acre smallholding in Llandwrog.

He got up from his chair, proceeded to place on his nose a pair of glasses which had definitely seen better days, took out of an inside pocket a rather grubby, folded cheque which he duly signed leaving me to complete the payee details (most farmers do this). He then signed the contract presented to him by Yappy, shook hands with all of us and left the hotel!

The one-man crowd, with few words but many twitches, was gone, leaving the two actors in this scarcely credible drama looking at one another, each beaming at a job well done, albeit so unexpectedly. I simply looked at both of them in sheer disbelief and admiration.

If this what the art of auctioneering was about, I had got rather a lot to learn!

Bugattis in Blaenau

Whenever I read any reference to a Bugatti motor car, I recall a visit made by Mack to Blaenau Ffestiniog (well, to Llan, actually) to see a client by the name of Hamish Moffat. The advantage of accompanying Mack on an assignment, particularly one as far as to Ffestiniog was that all Mack could do apart from concentrating on his driving was to talk. Each journey, in effect, became an instructional lecture on various aspects of auctioneering and estate agency. I could think of nothing better than to be mentored in this way. He talked and I listened, real one-to-one stuff which was brilliant.

We arrived at Mr Moffat's wonderfully remote, traditional Welsh cottage, in the hills above Llan, to be greeted by a young, dashing, man-about-town type who was charm personified and who, after all the usual polite preliminaries, proceeded to give us a guided tour of the property in order to be given an idea of its value. After the living accommodation came the boring part – the outbuildings and garage. But there was absolutely nothing remotely boring about the contents of this garage which, I do recall thinking, looked rather superior to most garages belonging to remote Welsh country cottages.

There, in all their total majesty stood, not one, but two gleaming, superbly restored and maintained Bugatti sports cars, one a type 35B and its partner a type 35T. Mack and I just stood there transfixed by the scene before us with both of us trying to comprehend the sheer incongruity of what stood before us, and my boss, with his finely-tuned business mind, trying to work out what these two magnificent machines might be worth. Whatever their value at that time, fifty years ago, will have totally paled into insignificance by today. I understand that very few 35Ts were produced at the time, which will further reflect the huge prices which these classics now command.

Hamish Moffat was to become one of the most flamboyant vintage racing enthusiasts of the 1960s and 70s with more than 200 trophies to his name. Not satisfied with speed on four wheels, Moffat later indulged a second passion – in the air, restoring and flying 1920s and 30s vintage aircraft and, occasionally, getting into some exciting scrapes with them.

In a way, this was a singularly unique day out for me. In Ffestiniog, North Wales, of all places, as opposed to the Cotswolds or to a desirable address in the Home Counties, I had been for the first, and only, time within touching distance, not of one, but of two, examples of one of the most famous and cherished classic car marques in the world. With due respect, the names Bugatti and Llan Ffestiniog are not normally the subject of sophisticated motoring-related conversation.

Violet Carson

I have to confess, if indeed a confession is required, to being a bit of a fan of the long-running 'soap' *Coronation Street*, which has been on our screens for at least fifty years. This has nothing directly to do with a brief anecdote I recall from the early 1960s whilst serving my articles with JP & Co., whose offices were prominently situated opposite the well-known, red brick town clock in the High Street flanked by the banks, Midland and Lloyds, in a position which today would be described as 'prime'.

At this time, we, the British population, were beginning to latch properly onto the merits and pleasures of television ownership, having put firmly behind us the late 1950s post-war austerity years. A television retail company based in the northwest was beginning to open outlets in the North Wales area. The Company was called Telefusion whose latest opening was to be a small corner shop unit right opposite J

P & Co.'s office by the town clock. Telefusion had hit on the idea of opening its new outlets with a degree of fanfare and had engaged the then, 'queen' of television, Violet Carson (aka Ena Sharples of *Coronation Street*) to perform the opening ceremony at all its new stores.

The local newspaper, the *Bangor Chronicle*, featured Violet Carson's impending visit thus ensuring considerable interest. Most of us in the office placed ourselves in the front first floor office window to view the proceedings. Miss Carson duly arrived in an open-topped car and anyone would have been forgiven for thinking that true royalty had made an appearance in Bangor that day, despite the relative newness of the *Coronation Street* soap.

Strife at Rhydwyn

Rhydwyn, a sleepy, peaceful village near Church Bay in the north of Anglesey, was not exactly renowned in the early 1960s for trouble and strife.

An uncle of mine (Glyndwr Rees) was a well-known and highly respected Baptist minister in the village, and in the late 1950s I can remember when on holiday there with my cousins, Rhydwyn was still reliant on the local pump for the inhabitants' daily supply of water.

The family's chapel house had not the luxury of a mains loo, just a 'one-seater' in a hut at the end of the back garden and when my uncle was called on to perform baptisms in the village, they took place in a stream running through a meadow near the chapel. A suitably deep baptism pool was very simply formed with two fairly substantial slate slabs which acted as dams for the duration of the ceremony.

Rhydwyn was, however, no different from other Anglesey rural villages at the time, when family strife decided to rear its ugly head. A very common scenario in farming communities, and Rhydwyn was no exception, was what I term the 'father/wife and sister/brother' scenario.

This is where a small farm or smallholding has been run reasonably successfully by the owner and his wife with a gradually increasing and necessary input from the so-far, unmarried son who lives at the property with his parents. Complicating the situation is the maiden daughter who also resides at the property. She does have a long-term, very long-term, boyfriend, who himself helps on his own family farm nearby.

Sadly, the father passes away, leaving the son very much in charge of the farming side of things with his sister left to see to the domestic tasks in place of a gradually failing mother who sadly passes on after her husband, leaving the brother and his sister as the sole beneficiaries of the farm and its everyday running.

The brother is still heavily involved on the farming side of things but his sister, having lost her mother, has now seen her domestic responsibilities virtually eliminated. She, understandably, now sees her position very much under threat, particularly as his input is now, far more important than that of hers. At all costs she must remain in occupation at the farm but all the time the relationship between brother and sister becomes extremely fraught.

In this particular instance, the brother/sister relationship very quickly became irreconcilable to the extent that solicitors acting for the respective parties were now very heavily involved in the increasingly sad situation. The whole tragic, and really unnecessary situation, escalated to the County Court and this is where John Pritchard & Co came on the scene.

In this instance, the Court directed that the whole domestic contents of the farm be sold by public auction with the net proceeds after expenses shared equally between brother and sister. So far, so good. The Court further directed that the auction had to take place within one calendar month, so there was not a lot of time to waste.

Derek Goodwin, Mack's assistant and right-hand man, decreed that three of us – himself and the two 'learners,' Jeremy Jones and yours truly, should visit Rhydwyn as early as possible, but giving both the sister and her brother due notice of our intended visit.

An early start was duly decided upon. Unlike the present main A5 highway (Bangor to Holyhead in sixteen minutes), Rhydwyn was not exactly one of the quickest places to reach along the old back road through Llangefni and Bodedern before hitting the top road leading from Valley to Cemaes Bay. Derek's trusty green Morris Minor Estate with wooden panels and no such thing as power steering, would get us there in no fewer than forty-five minutes on a good day.

We arrived at the smallholding with some trepidation, not knowing the degree of hostility we might, quite understandably, be shown by either or, indeed, both of the litigants. It became apparent, however, that both sister and brother had been warned by their respective legal representatives to behave themselves and to give the auctioneers the maximum help and co-operation during the whole time of our visit to the property.

Derek led us on a brief tour of the property to get our bearings and to take in visually just what was involved. It became quickly apparent that the relatively small rooms were going to render an auction of the contents inside the house a virtual impossibility. On our way in, Derek had spotted a large, well-maintained shed close to the back door of the house and a quick inspection told us immediately that this would be the place to hold the auction, despite the need to remove everything from within the house onto tables in the shed prior to their being suitably lotted and catalogued.

Without doubt, this task alone would take us the best part of a day plus all the lotting-time required. So, a plan of campaign was hatched there and then and related to the sister and brother, so that they were both absolutely clear as to the nature of our plan of action.

We were to return to the farm two days later at the crack of dawn and in the meantime we would be preparing advertisements announcing the auction in the local *Herald Mon* and *Holyhead and Anglesey Mail* newspapers. So, it was now 'game on' as they say.

The other crucial direction of the Court was that pending the final outcome of the case, the sister and brother were to immediately vacate the house despite the wish of, and indeed, the necessity for the brother to continue farming the holding and to keep it in tidy order. We retained a key to the farmhouse and one for the 'auction building,' and assumed that the matter of the vacation of the farmhouse by the sister and brother was one for the respective solicitors, and not for any of us to worry about.

We made the return journey to Rhydwyn as planned two days later and spent the whole of the day doing the carrying from the house and the sorting in the building in such a way that Mack with his critical eye for detail would have little or no cause to question our auction-arranging ability. We completed our task much later on that day and left the 'auction shed' looking just as the Boss would have expected, before commencing the return journey to Bangor. The auction was duly advertised to take place some two weeks later on a Friday at 1 pm with viewing to commence at, as I recall, 10 am.

The intervening two weeks to the auction date soon sped by and suddenly, the Friday auction day saw our making an early, and final journey to Rhydwyn for this rather unusual and, in many ways, sad and unnecessary auction. Derek, Jeremy and I all left Bangor together early on the Friday so as to arrive in Rhydwyn well before the viewing public and to cast our eyes over any final, minor details. Mack would arrive under his own steam nearer the auction start time.

We arrived at the farm to find the place quiet and deserted which was the very scenario we had been expecting bearing in mind the circumstances which had occasioned the proposed auction in the first place. One of us casually unlocked the 'auction shed' door. It was not only absolutely empty, but cleaned and swept out too! We stared, firstly at one another, and then around the shed, expecting to see all our hard work reappear as if by magic. But reappear it did not and we just continued staring at each other in absolute disbelief!

What on earth would Mack have to say about a situation which he, doubtless, in all his years as an auctioneer, would not have previously encountered? Someone, I cannot recall who, decided to pop into the farmhouse, possibly half expecting to see someone there. there was no-one, but the second profound shock of the morning was to hit us – every single item removed so carefully by us to the 'auction shed' had been equally carefully returned, it seemed, to the farmhouse, each piece reinstated back to its original position as if it had never been anywhere else!

Decisions, very quick ones, clearly had to be made by someone, bearing in mind that the viewing public would be starting to turn up very soon. 'Public' Auctions are exactly what it says on the tin – 'Public' – and the problem is that if the auctioneer does not get his arrangements right on the day then the 'public' soon gets to hear of those failings regardless of the fact that such failings may have been totally out of the auctioneer's hands, as was clearly the case here in Rhydwyn.

The decision was made to allow the viewing of the sale lots in the house itself, but clearly there was no question of being able to hold the auction there as well. So, we would proceed to remove from the house to the shed as many lots as were required to commence the auction and as the auction proceeded under Mack's hammer, the rest of us would continue 'feeding' further items, in lot order, from the house until all lots had been placed, for the second time, back to where they had been originally intended. Mercifully, all went well with buyers barely noticing that there had been anything untoward. There were, however, one or two comments from the local populace to the effect that we had been lucky to have been able to conduct the auction at all in view of the simmering trouble within the family which was described as a 'family war' waiting to happen.

We never did get to find out which of the protagonists had caused us such extra work and inconvenience on that day, but many weeks later, in County Court proceedings to resolve the family dispute, both brother and sister were publicly criticised by the judge and although words such as 'contempt' were suggested, a line was apparently drawn over the potential fiasco of the auction day which had been unusual and quite eventful, to say the very least!

2

Caernarfon
1963–1967

I suppose that, in a way, my departure from John Pritchard & Co. in 1963, having completed my three years' articles, was a slightly strange parting of the ways. Mack had not indicated any wish for me to remain; perhaps he just assumed that I would. For my part, I think there was the feeling of Articles having been completed and that therefore it was time to seek pastures new. Whilst I had certainly benefitted from Mack's three years' crash course in the rudiments of auctioneering and estate agency, I felt that I had also played my part by giving it my all during that period of intense training.

Bob Parry & Co., the powerful agricultural and property auctioneers with their head office in Caernarfon, were advertising for an 'assistant to the property manager'. The company had recently taken on a new managing director, R. G. Pritchard-Jones, a dashing young product of Cardiganshire whose appointment had ruffled a feather or two as there was felt to be ample existing talent within the company to fill the post.

The company directors were, by and large, 'yes' men from the farming community, so that the new MD required very little time to have them eating out of the proverbial hand. He very soon proved to the local agricultural populace what an authoritative and powerful auctioneer he was. During this period in the 1960s Bob Parry & Company were the 'kings' of the North Wales livestock market scene. Whilst their principal market was in Llangefni, the company operated numerous 'satellite' markets at Valley, Anglesey and at Llanrwst, Bryncir and Pwllheli on the mainland.

Additionally, there were occasional markets including Tŷ Croes and Menai Bridge on Anglesey and Sarn, Tal-y-cafn and, in earlier times, Conwy on the mainland. In later years, Pritchard-Jones, in his infinite wisdom, was to realize the futility of operating so many livestock markets so geographically close to one another, particularly with the vastly improved transport links throughout the North Wales area.

I duly attended an interview with Pritchard-Jones and was delighted to be offered the advertised post at what I thought was the princely salary of £1000 per annum. It was at that point that I felt that my departure from Bangor had been a shrewd move. I was to be an assistant on the estate agency side to the property manager LTO (Tecwyn) Thomas and to be involved in any chattels auctions that happened to come along. Tecwyn was a fully qualified chartered surveyor for whom 'selling houses' was felt to be a job anyone could really do. The 'professional work' was the real deal, in his eyes – land management, compensation claims, arbitrations and the like.

I was very soon introduced to a member of staff shortly to retire after many years with the company, Mr Owain Maldwyn Roberts. He was a lovely, red-faced, kindly man who, soon after being introduced, used to greet 20-year-old me, rather disarmingly, as 'Mister' Rogers Jones. Mr Roberts was, without any doubt, the 1960s version of a twenty first century computer. He had an absolutely infallible photographic memory of the minutest details relating to properties which he had been involved with and sold over a great number of years.

Not only details of the bricks and mortar side of things but the name of the owner, how long he or she had resided there, who the husband or wife was and where their place of work happened to be etc. But it did not always stop there; he would often quote the name of an owner previous to the present client and how much the property had sold for all those years ago!

I would return to the office having begun visiting properties to take details unaccompanied. "Where have we been today, Mr Rogers Jones?" he would ask, in his usual cordial manner.

I would quote a property I had just visited, whereupon Mr Roberts would begin a potted history of the particular house and at the same time, just to verify his facts, he would proceed to open one of the drawers of a neat little wooden filing cabinet which contained the hand-written details of all the properties he'd been involved with over so many years! He was not only a lovely man but surely Caernarfon's property encyclopaedia as well! Who needs computers?

Having secured the post in Caernarfon, I now had to secure somewhere to live there, as I had no intention of making the daily, pre-A55 journey from my parents' house in Llandudno Junction where my father ran his business of dispensing chemist

How it came about, I cannot recall, but lodgings were secured for me with the Williams family in Segontium Terrace, most handily placed a matter of yards from Bob Parry's office in Castle Square. Mr and Mrs Williams, their young son and her elderly parents hailed from one of the Caernarfon quarrying villages (Rhosgadfan, I think) and Mr Williams was one of the town's team of postmen.

It was a homely, friendly household. I ate with the family and had my own room on the second floor at the front overlooking the harbour. The old couple were lovely; every day I would be greeted with *"Sut ath hi heddiw?"* (How did it go today?). We'd chat about all I'd done that day and they showed genuine interest. He was semi-housebound so that the television was a source of constant entertainment. I remember that the old man's most favourite programme was the American detective series Perry Mason, except that he always referred to it as 'Parry' Mason, which was guaranteed to crease me every time!

My Very First 'Own' Auction

Instructions were received one routine day to conduct a farm, or in this particular case, a smallholding dispersal sale, at Cefn Ynysoedd Bach Llanfaglan, a short car ride away from the Caernarfon Office.

This was to be my debut sale for Bob Parry & Co., disposing of the house contents in the open air in the yard of the holding after all the 'proper' auctioneering of the hens, a few cows and pigs as well as the modest collection of farm machinery, had taken place.

In the 60s, this was the way of the world – a sale on the premises in the open air, take a chance on the weather and there you are! Any removal of such a relatively small number of household items to another venue, assuming one to be available, was totally and uneconomically out of the question. All the items for sale, including the fairly modest bedroom furniture, had been moved into the small yard area close to the house with all the china, glassware, metalware and other bric-a-brac laid out on trestle tables.

The sheer informality of the occasion was quite refreshing compared with the rather clinical orderliness of today's auctions. Farmers' wives, many in regulation headscarves and overcoats, crowded round the tables and after a quick introduction and a brief reference to the conditions of sale, I got the proceedings going with few, if any, of the customers realizing that this was DRJ's debut auction!

*My first farm auction at Cefn Ynysoedd,
Llanfaglan, August 1964*

As I have no recollection of any problems or backlash following my debut auction at Llanfaglan, I think I can safely assume that proceedings went reasonably well.

Auction at Plas Brereton

One of the senior members of staff at Bob Parry & Company during my time there was John Morus Jones, or, 'John Moi,' as he was affectionately known to all. John lived with his young family at nearby Bontnewydd and held a most unusual position within the Bob Parry & Co. hierarchy.

I recall the story that he had been extremely disappointed at having lost out in his application to be Managing Director of the company to the young, handsome raider from Mid Wales, R G Pritchard-Jones, who was awarded this most prestigious of posts, following, as it did, that held by the patriarch of the company, John Ivor Jones.

Bob Parry's premises were situated most prominently right on 'Y Maes' (or Castle Square) in the centre of town a short distance from the famous castle. Right next door to the auctioneers was the equally prestigious premises of the local newspaper, the Caernarfon & Denbigh Herald. No problem there, the reader might assume; except for two highly unusual factors.

Firstly, John was the Managing Director and, effectively, the owner, of the Herald group of newspapers. Secondly, the group not only owned its printing premises and headquarters on 'Y Maes' but the adjoining premises occupied by Bob Parry & Co. as well. 'John Moi' was therefore the landlord of premises occupied by his employers, and was never to lose the hurt felt at having lost out to Mr Pritchard-Jones for the directorship of the auctioneering company who were his tenants at their Caernarfon headquarters. A highly unusual business situation!

John busied himself mainly on the professional, land and agricultural side of things and had a wide client base. I think it would be fair to say that the actual auctioning side of things occupied second place in his preferences and so it was that he came along to me one day asking me to accompany him to premises on the outskirts of Caernarfon in order to take a preliminary look. John was a past master of the 'mock-posh' form of address, hence the rather extravagant emphasis on the 'Mister' as he set out for my benefit where we were about to visit.

Our destination was Plas Brereton, a 19th Century, detached gentleman's residence situated within its own walled boundary right on the main Bangor road leading out of Caernarfon. John's tasks ahead of him were to be exclusively on the property side with mine on the contents of the property.

In relating this anecdote, I fully realise that these were very early days in my career as an auctioneer and that, therefore, any new assignment might give me an exaggerated impression of every task that came my way. But what I was about to witness in this house in 1965 was truly quite remarkable, the details of which I remember quite vividly over fifty years later.

Plas Brereton was the classic time-warp situation. Every single item inside the house shouted the 1900s – a true step back in time, with everything from the curtains, carpets, furnishings, kitchen utensils and even redundant foodstuffs all from a bygone era. From these contents it would have been an easy matter to draw up a comprehensive catalogue of home furnishings and utensils available in that era. The cellars of the house even contained dust-covered bottles of quality champagne, but I seem to recall that John 'took charge' of those!

As soon as all this had been taken in, I busied myself with organizing a sort-out of the contents preparatory to an auction to be held on the premises. Very soon, the local press, presumably encouraged by John, began to show interest in the forthcoming auction and this was very much a new insight for me – the local press involved in a public auction which, in itself was good for both the auction itself and the company in charge of proceedings.

The day of the auction duly arrived; not only had local advertisements brought in potential purchasers and the inevitable number of spectators from far and wide but the television cameras too; and to all of us involved in this wonderful auction, the very presence of the cameras served to highlight what was, at the time, a particularly important event.

Looking back to the auction at Plas Brereton, the strange factor to consider, over fifty years after the auction took place, is that the contents of the house, at the time of that memorable event, were a relatively young sixty-four years old, and yet the feeling of stepping back in time to the 1900s was, in my recollection, a much, much more, mind-boggling one.

Caernarfon Joker

One fairly routine morning, I was on my way out of the office and proceeded downstairs – our offices were on the first floor of the property with the reception office near the entrance on the ground floor – when I hit upon a conversation between a young Caernarfon girl who had commenced her very first post with us two days previously, and a slightly portly gentleman customer who was leaning over her desk begging her earnest concentration.

I stopped on the stairs to hear a conversation which went along the following lines: "You've probably been made aware that all new employees at Bob Parry & Company have to enroll within seven days as summer volunteers with haymaking assistance during the harvest in Cesarea". Not only did this seem strange per se, but I felt it rather strange that Cesarea, a very elevated quarrying village with little, or no, haymaking potential, should be the subject of such officialdom.

The new recruit listened intently and nervously and even began jotting down brief notes whilst taking in all the complex-sounding details. The 'interview' eventually ended with the gentleman declaring that "he would be along with the final details in a few days' time."

As I proceeded quietly down the two or three remaining steps, I caught sight of the gentleman turning towards the door and proffering a sly wink in the direction of another member of staff who, I strongly suspect, knew exactly what was going on!

Of course there was no haymaking in Cesarea, of all places, and certainly there was no scheme to enlist volunteers for such a hair-brained idea!

This was my first introduction to Ritchie Bonner-Pritchard, businessman and practical joker 'of this parish.'

R B-P, as I shall refer to him, with his brother, ran an old-established and highly reputable furniture removal business in the town, Pritchard Brothers, Porth yr Aur. If you'd moved house into, or out of, Caernarfon, the chances are that you will have had this firm moving you in their gentle, polite, old-fashioned way. The business was continued very successfully in subsequent years by R B-P's two nephews, John and David until they retired in 2011. David, or 'Diddy,' as he was affectionately known, sadly passed away in 2013.

How R B-P managed to successfully combine the running of his business whilst at the same time causing absolute hilarity with his elaborate practical joking, is quite beyond me. I suppose that if practical joking is regarded as an art form, then I have been privileged to witness one of the finest exponents of that skill.

One quiet routine morning, I was in Castle Square and realized that, unwittingly I had come across the preliminaries to one of R B-P's practical jokes.

He was standing outside the impressive façade of the National Provincial Bank (the Nat. West today), looking very official with a clipboard in one hand and a tape measure in the other. He took his time in 'assessing' his potential victims as they went about their normal daily business; R B-P knew that he had to choose an innocent stranger to the town rather than one of the locals who were so familiar with his antics.

A victim was chosen. "Excuse me sir, I wonder if you would help me. I'm a local surveyor and I have to measure the frontage of this bank but my assistant is away today so I could just do with a hand to hold one end of the tape. Do you think you could oblige? It won't take a moment and I'd be most grateful," continued R B-P in his most persuasive manner.

"Yes, of course", replied the willing victim, "what would you like me to do?"

Profusely thanking him for his readiness to help, R B-P took him along the side of the bank and instructed his new assistant to hold the end of the measuring tape in a certain position on the wall. R B-P then took the other end round to the front of the bank out of his victim's sight and proceeded to tie his end of the tape to a drain pipe that was quite used to this sort of thing. R B-P would then retreat to his favourite corner on 'Y Maes' to witness the poor victim's ever-changing demeanour from wrist-watch looking, to slight exasperation, to worry and finally to downright annoyance on being told by passers-by that he had become yet another R B-P victim!

Topping the 'outrageous' scale by a clear mile, was one of R B-P's other practical jokes. He would stalk Castle Square for his victims, preferably, for this occasion, a couple of obvious visitors to the town. Another vital part of the plan had already been sorted. The victims were approached. "Pardon me, are you visiting this historic old town? If so, as a proud resident born and bred here, I should be thrilled and delighted if you would allow me to give you a brief trip in my car just to acquaint you with some of the main attractions; we'll only be five minutes or so."

"What a kind man", was the immediate reaction, whose generous offer was taken up without hesitation. "Just give me five minutes whilst I pop to the bank over there; follow me to my car, make yourselves comfortable and I'll be with you shortly".

Five minutes went by, then ten, by which time R B-P had taken up his strategic position on the other side of The

Square, just in time to see the car's owner turn up and who could barely contain himself on seeing two complete strangers occupying the rear seat of his beloved motor vehicle! R B-P stayed around just long enough to witness at a distance the arm waving and finger pointing which went on between the two parties!

The reader may throw hands up in horror at such childish pranks perpetrated by an adult but it is worth remembering that this was the gentler, slightly more innocent 1960s when road rage, neighbours from hell and Asbos had not, thankfully, been invented!

1965 and Marriage

Life at Bob Parry & Co. zoomed along quite merrily. In a way I felt it to be a positive advantage that the company did not run its own furniture saleroom, thus giving me flexibility to learn other important facets of the business.

All the livestock auctioneers had immense experience but they were just that – livestock auctioneers with few other strings to their bows. I tried to concentrate on the estate agency side of the business, but with any furniture auctions which came along being an added bonus. I continued lodging happily in Segontium Terrace until, one day in 1964, I had a sudden brainwave. Why not get married to my long-time girl-friend Margaret, who qualified as a radiographer in the oncology department at Clatterbridge Hospital on the Wirral?

Whilst she was on the verge of completing her training, the rather specialised nature of her calling meant that Margaret was unlikely to get a post in our area, dealing specifically in the subject she had trained and qualified in.

We fixed a date for our wedding for the end of February 1965 and in the meantime Margaret obtained a post in the electronics department of Bangor University. We also managed to cobble together finance towards the purchase of a delightful ex-quarryman's cottage high up on the hillside at Fachwen, overlooking Llanberis Lake. Pant Gwyn cost all of £1,700 which was exactly £700 more than my then annual salary at Bob Parry & Co!

We were duly married at Conwy and spent a wonderful week's honeymoon in sunny Cornwall, where it was very strange to hear on the national news that 'due to the very heavy snowstorms in North Wales, businesses and council offices in Caernarfon had closed early due to traffic disruption, and children had been sent home from school.' Our arrival back at our new home in Fachwen was particularly memorable in that we had to park the car at the entrance end of the narrow lane to Pant Gwyn and walk to the cottage along the tops of the walls due to the height of the snowdrifts!

Routine was quickly re-established at the office, soon after which we received instructions to conduct an in-house auction of the contents of a nice house in Llanwnda, a short distance from Caernarfon. One of the highlights of these contents was a very nicely preserved oak Welsh dresser, with a matching press cupboard made by the same craftsman. It immediately occurred to me how well these two pieces would look in our new marital home.

As I would be conducting the auction, I deemed it ethically necessary to inform Mr Pritchard-Jones of my interest in this lot and he kindly arranged for another member of staff to bid on the items on my behalf. I was thrilled to be the successful purchaser of the dresser and cupboard for the princely sum of £45.

I duly made arrangements for the transport of the items to Pant Gwyn, little realising the trouble that lay ahead. In my rush and enthusiasm to furnish our new cottage home with these lovely pieces I had not given a second's thought to one very important logistical detail. The driver of the van I had engaged to transport the valuable cargo all the way from Llanwnda to Fachwen soon realised on arrival at the cottage that a Welsh dresser 6 foot 8 inches high was going to be rather difficult to fit into the room of a quarryman's cottage with a beamed ceiling 6 foot 6 inches high!

Neither the dresser nor its partner, the press cupboard, as much as stepped over the threshold of our new home! The sequel to this story was that we had to start again with our plans to furnish Pant Gwyn, but we were extremely lucky in one respect – a friend of ours in Porthmadog agreed to take the furniture off us for the price we had given at the auction. Phew!

If an auctioneer could commit such a basic error, it did not augur well for any potential buying customers!

In the 1960s, Bob Parry & Co. was very much an expanding, rather than a contracting, business, particularly on the property side of the organization. A new estate office was opened in a good position in Porthmadog and I was detailed to visit this new office on a regular basis, once a week at least, to try and assist in drumming up new business in a town and environs which were already well served by established estate agents of good repute.

I began to visit 'Port' every Friday and I have to state that it was quite a relief to get out of the head office in Caernarfon on a regular basis as there persisted a somewhat gloomy atmosphere in the property department there.

No sooner had I settled down to my 'Port on Friday' routine, than I received a 'summons' from the best Nain in the world – my grandmother on my mother's side, a long-time resident of nearby Criccieth – to go over to her house for my Friday lunch.

Nain was the liveliest grandmother imaginable; ardent chapel-goer at Lloyd George's Seion Chapel opposite her terraced house and a landlady who let the top part of her home to summer visitors. She must have been popular to have let her flat to the same family from Walsall, Staffordshire for a continuous seventeen years.

Oh, and I nearly forgot – she was also a wonderful cook. I don't mean a chef or other fancy description, just a good, old-fashioned cook of simple, wholesome ingredients. More extraordinary is the fact that all her wonderful concoctions were produced on a good old style Baby Belling cooker – you know the type if you're of a certain age – a box-like white enamel affair not much larger than one of today's microwave ovens and having two cooking plates on top, one round and one oblong.

Complementing the Belling in the living room was an old fashioned steel fire range, black-leaded and polished till you could see your face in it. My Friday lunch became a much-to-look-forward-to affair and was invariably haddock or cod with mash and garden peas followed by a simply divine, light-as-a-feather, apple suet pudding with white sauce. We both enjoyed our regular Friday lunchtimes, she for the chat and I for both the chat and Nain's lovely food.

Most of us at some time or other have been asked the question "where were you when…?" I shall never forget the Friday I made my regular lunchtime visit to Criccieth on 21st October 1966. Nain did not appear to be her usual cheerful self and proceeded to tell me about the dreadful avalanche disaster which had befallen Aberfan at a quarter past nine that morning.

This was my first news of the catastrophe and I have to say that this was the one and only time when lunch at Nain's turned out to be a rather subdued affair. Nothing very much was said between us that lunchtime as we listened to the dreadful news on her trusty Murphy radio.

3

Harlech and Hereford
1967–1968

After three interesting years and a good deal of profitable experience, I began to have itchy feet once again. My weekly visits to Porthmadog and to Criccieth for my lunch on a Friday led me to the possibility of settling down on the beautiful Cambrian coast. I was also becoming somewhat discouraged by the distinctive lack of ambiance and encouragement in the Caernarfon property department.

An estate agent based in Aberdyfi, N P S Winfield, was advertising for an assistant to manage a new property office in Harlech. Without enquiring very much regarding the repute and stability of this man's business, I said a rather impetuous "yes" to his offer of a post as his manager, whereupon Margaret and I placed Pant Gwyn on the market, after giving Mr Pritchard-Jones due notice of my intention to leave Caernarfon.

Sometime during that period of notice, I was approached in the office by one of the firm's directors, Mr Vincent Oliver, a former local bank manager and, by then, an excellent and experienced director and ambassador for Bob Parry and Co. Without preamble of any sort, I was asked a very direct question as to whether I was absolutely certain that I was doing the right thing in joining a small business of limited and hitherto unproven repute.

Mr Oliver went so far as to hint that he'd made his own enquiries regarding Winfield and was evidently not impressed by what he'd discovered. I think that I rather flattered myself into thinking that the sole motive for Mr Oliver's intervention was to dissuade me from leaving the company. On reflection, not long afterwards, I was to feel that he had been simply offering helpful advice with no ulterior motive at all.

So that was it, we were on our way to Harlech, to a small modern bungalow occupying a superb position overlooking everywhere and just a short distance from the village.

A 1960s bungalow, Awel y Mynydd had a black and yellow bathroom suite. Ugh! It had been built by a young local couple, the Stewarts, who had moved to another property over the road and with whom amongst others, we became good friends; there was also an impressively large garden with two greenhouses which would have been marvellous except for one thing – I wasn't particularly fond of gardening!

Pant Gwyn found a new owner very quickly – a well-known television culinary personality – and so our new adventure, not too many miles down the road, had begun in earnest. Soon, it was down to work for yours truly at the new office in Harlech; settling in and organising things meant a busy and satisfying period but it was some time before anything like decent numbers of property instructions came my way. Like it or not, what I was not going to receive in any numbers at all were instructions to conduct furniture auctions which, after all, was what I had been trained for, and which I was naturally keen to pursue. I kept my head down, nevertheless, and began to nurture some good contacts with solicitors with whom I had not had previous dealings whilst in Porthmadog.

However, several months into my tenure in Harlech, I began to witness a rather disturbing development. Two property transactions which I had successfully negotiated were due for completion by the solicitors. The 10 per cent

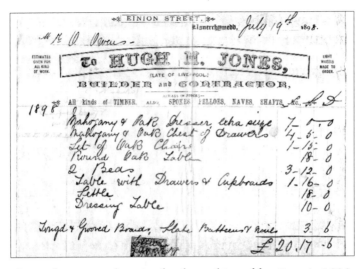

Copy of an original receipt for the making of furniture in 1898.

deposit paid on one of the transactions was due for release to the solicitors by Winfield, less our charges. He, Winfield, had sole responsibility for this as the accounts for all the branches were controlled from the main office in Aberdyfi.

Despite repeated requests from the solicitors through me, the balance deposit was not forthcoming, increasing my anger and embarrassment with each passing hour. The solicitors, to their credit, and to my considerable relief, absolved me from any blame for this situation, in return for which I undertook to report the matter to the professional body of which Winfield was a member.

I received from them a prompt and sympathetic response but also the strong advice that I should seek a post elsewhere before, and just in case, people's anger began to be directed towards me personally.

This advice was duly chewed over by Margaret and me and it was with some regret that we agreed that our stay in this lovely part of North Wales was going to be far shorter than we had originally intended. This sad decision rather overshadowed our joyful news that Margaret was expecting our first baby but we began, almost immediately, to seek out any posts on offer in any part of the country, within reason, although the nearer to our 'home patch' the better.

Home or Away?

I referred earlier to the dominance of Bob Parry & Co. as agricultural auctioneers with its blanket coverage of livestock markets and offices throughout the region. In 1964 this dominance was to be shaken by a ground-breaking decision arrived at by one man. His name – Morgan Evans. For something like seventeen years Morgan had given skilful and faithful service as an auctioneer to his bosses in Caernarfon, but his youthful ambition was pointing him firmly in a direction which was to raise eyebrows throughout the North Wales agricultural community.

Morgan had made the momentous decision to leave Bob Parry & Co. in order to open, and operate, his own livestock market at Gaerwen on Anglesey. This decision shook his employers in Caernarfon to the core; indeed an immediate attempt was made to invoke a 'restraint of trade' condition on him which would have prevented him from opening premises within certain previously agreed distances from his employers' operating bases.

So important was the issue that Morgan engaged his solicitor and an eminent barrister to fight his corner and challenge the very constraining clauses to which he had agreed. Evidently realising that they had a serious fight on their hands and that public opinion in the form of many of their own customers was against them, Bob Parry & Co. relented, whereupon Morgan continued with his ambitious plans to alter the face of livestock auctioning on Anglesey.

In the meantime, the talk amongst the sceptical Island farming community was about one thing only. Indeed, I have heard it said that bets were being laid, not only on the likelihood of the failure of Morgan's plans but also as to the length of time this seemingly crazy venture was going to last. But no one had considered the determination of this man and how well he had honed his business skills whilst with Bob Parry & Co. Failure was definitely not on Morgan's agenda and the rest is history.

Coinciding with our problems in Harlech, I had been given a tip that an approach to Morgan Evans offering my services as an assistant, might be just what we were looking for, thus keeping us in the area we were both so familiar with.

An approach was duly made and with bated breath we awaited a response. It soon came but was not what we wanted to hear; on the advice of his accountants it was felt that Morgan's new business was not quite in a sufficiently healthy financial position to take an assistant on. And so it was back to the drawing board for the two of us!

Very soon, I was made aware of two posts for an auctioneer's assistant on offer in the national press. Good news, except that one was in Gloucester and the other in Hereford. I attended interviews for both. The Gloucester post was with Bruton Knowles, whose senior partner was the well-known and iconic Arthur Negus of early *Antiques Roadshow* fame. The other was with F H Sunderland & Co. who operated the livestock market in Hereford and who had a prominently situated estate office in the town. I accepted the latter's post of assistant to the property manager, Bill Rollings, and soon we were on our way to Hereford, having given due notice to Winfield and my reasons for doing so.

Awel y Mynydd was disposed of quickly, but rather sadly, as we had anticipated settling down in that lovely area for a good long spell. We swapped it for a very 'standard modern semi' (three bedrooms, a garage and central heating) in a residential area close to Hereford town centre. It cost us all of £4,000 and I suppose that we both felt fairly relieved at being able to walk straight out of one post into another, particularly with a baby on the way.

We soon experienced our first Herefordshire winter with very heavy snowfalls but I seemed to be the only one around able to manage the conditions with my lovely, metal-bottomed Mini Cooper which just left a flattened pack of snow in its wake! We paid frequent visits to our families back home and the journey soon became a very easy one. I was enjoying working under Bill Rollings, who was popular not only with the staff at Sunderlands, but with all of his clients also.

However, it soon became fairly clear to me that any appearances on the furniture rostrum were going to be fairly limited, as the auctioneer incumbent in that role was fairly forthcoming with his declaration that he did not intend having his pitch queered by some upstart from 'up north'. We saw our first winter through and our thoughts inevitably turned to the momentous and scary event which was to take place in May – the birth of our first child.

As the date neared, little did either of us think how significant the word 'scary' was going to turn out to be. Margaret was booked into the Hereford County Hospital for the birth.

Such was the appalling, indecisive treatment she received there, one would be forgiven for thinking that this was 1868 and not, as it was, 1968! After a totally unnecessary and ridiculously prolonged labour, Shân Elinor, all nine and a half pounds of her, came into the world as an English daughter of Welsh parents! In today's litigation-obsessed era, there is little doubt that Hereford County Hospital would have been required to answer some serious questions regarding the standard of treatment that Margaret received.

Her awful travails were, however, soon forgotten as we settled down in our modern semi as a threesome and continued enjoying and familiarizing ourselves with Hereford and its lovely environs.

Chinese Beds in Hereford

A very good client of Sunderlands, with both commercial and private properties in Hereford, which the company managed for him, had a problem. He reported to one of the directors, with whom he was very friendly on a social basis, his suspicions that an apartment located above one of his shops in the centre of town, had rather more occupiers in it than had been officially agreed in the tenancy agreement. The apartment was let to a very nice married Chinese couple together with her sister and brother.

It was agreed with the tenants for an official inspection of the property to be carried out by the landlord and us as his agents, in order to get to the bottom of what appeared to be a fairly simple problem or misunderstanding. The inspection duly commenced, three of us from the office looking suitably 'official' in Sunday suits which made us look more akin to tax inspectors than estate agents. In we all trooped, to be given the politest of greetings by the tenants and to find the lounge, kitchen bathroom and the first of the three bedrooms all in order.

This was proving to be an easy inspection so far but as one of us made to open the door of the second bedroom, Mr Chinese person rushed forward to say "I very sorry, this bedroom locked, I no have key, key with my wife's brother, he away for the day".

Strange, was our reaction, but on we proceeded to look at the third bedroom. All in order – no problem there.

In view of the slightly incomplete inspection, it was agreed with the tenants that the apartment would be revisited the following day, time deliberately unspecified, in order to see the somewhat mysteriously locked third bedroom.

The three of us repeated our visit to the apartment the following day to receive from the occupiers, once again, a repeat of the previous day's politest of welcomes.

It really was hard to conceive that anything mysterious was likely to be found with these gentle, polite tenants. We made a beeline for the previously locked third bedroom; in we went – all in order – except for one thing, or rather, except for eight things – the tell-tale signs of the indentations of two sets of four bed-legs in the fitted carpet!

We looked at one another without commenting, but one of us decided, on a whim, to ask for a quick second look inside the first bedroom which we had found to be in order the previous day.

Once again from Mr Chinese person – "I very sorry again, this bedroom locked, I unable to find the key at the moment".

By now, notwithstanding the polite co-operation of the tenants, we were slowly beginning to have our suspicions about them, plus mounting anger at what we felt to be the mickey-taking, time-wasting tactics on their part. Were they innocents or all-knowing conspirators in this seemingly comical scenario?

An impromptu conference was held on the landing of the apartment out of earshot of the tenants and it was unanimously decided to tell them, quite firmly, that we intended calling yet again the following day and that we expected all rooms in the apartment to be available for a full and thorough inspection.

We duly called the following day as arranged, somewhat fed up by now with a task that had taken far more time than had been allowed for. "Are all the bedrooms open?" we asked on arrival. No verbal replies were proffered by Mr Chinese person, just a rapid succession of head nods and a demeanour which suggested that the family had been well and truly found out.

Into all the three unlocked bedrooms we proceeded, whereupon our suspicions were finally confirmed. Bedroom one, the largest, had no fewer than three sets of four bed-leg indentations in the carpet with identical numbers in the third bedroom. It took only a very quick calculation to determine that this family of four persons, including Mr and Mrs Chinese persons as a married couple, had no fewer than eight beds in this three-bedroomed apartment. So who, and where, were these extra bed-occupiers?

It transpired that the two sons of Mr and Mrs Chinese persons and their wives ran a restaurant in town, a short distance away; the couples had four young children between them, making ten in all, and who, between them, were responsible for all those suspicious indentations in the carpets.

Whilst talking idly with an assistant in a nearby shop, the young lady quite casually expressed surprise that over the past three days, there had been some incredibly frequent movements of beds both in, and out, of the apartment and she really could not make out why.

Sorting beds out in Hereford can take a heck of a lot of valuable time but rather reluctantly, I had to concede a slight degree of ingenuity on the part of our Chinese tenants!

A Very Unexpected Summons

Life in Hereford proceeded quite satisfactorily with my enthusiasm for work very much back on track after the trauma of Shân's arrival, and boosted by having conducted two good furniture auctions in recent weeks, albeit due primarily to the illness of Sunderlands' incumbent chattels auctioneer.

The late spring and early summer weather took us out to the lovely Herefordshire countryside on as many occasions as possible, as well as journeys back home in order to show off the new arrival to doting grandparents. Neighbours on our modern estate were a very friendly lot but with a new baby, forming social connections was not an easy task, so there was a natural inclination to keep ourselves to ourselves.

After one routine working day, the three of us were settling down to some summer evening leisure time when the telephone rang. The call ended and I returned to where Margaret was seated, barely able to get the words out to tell her who the caller was.

Eventually, I managed to blurt out that it was Morgan Evans asking if I was interested in joining him as an assistant on Anglesey. Having been rejected for the same post for very sound business reasons only nine months previously, it was with some degree of frustration and bewilderment that Margaret and I had to sit down and talk rather urgently about this new, but potentially exciting, development.

I just could not work out my emotion and response to this news. Was it one of elation at the prospects on offer or one of utter annoyance that we were only less than a year down the line after a move to Hereford and the purchase of a house and all that it entailed?

I do remember misguidedly giving the potential problem of selling the house in what, at the time, was a rather static property market, more head-scratching than the potential of the post in Anglesey itself.

In the cold light of the following day, the decision we now had to make really was an easy one and so we made it; there was a simple sequence of things to do – accept Morgan's offer of the post, inform my employers of the decision and place our home of just nine months, on the market as quickly as possible.

The formalities with Morgan Evans were soon concluded and the directors of Sunderlands, to their credit, showed a commendable understanding of the situation. The summer months soon sped by with September 1968 the agreed time for our move back up north. The office in Hereford took on the task of trying to dispose of the house and to our very great relief a customer was found with surprising speed.

Nine months previously, we had paid exactly £4,000 for our modern semi and to our great delight an offer of £4,100 was received, and quickly accepted. Looking back, it is hard to believe that we felt so much relief at having actually made a profit of £100 on a property transaction in such a short space of time.

We departed Hereford without really getting to know it, or its people properly, which was a great shame but looking back, there is no doubt that the magnets of our North Wales roots were far too strong to resist.

4

Anglesey
1968–1992

We managed a surprisingly smooth departure from Hereford, albeit with a certain degree of regret that our stay had been so short and rather unfulfilled. The sale of our house there concluded quickly, allowing us to purchase an almost-completed new bungalow in Llanfairpwll. Obtaining a mortgage in the 1960s was slightly less fraught than frustrating hurdles and difficulties which poor house-seekers experience today. It was amazing for us to realise that in exactly four years, Margaret and I had purchased, and disposed of, three properties and that as we made this move to Anglesey in 1968, we were only twenty-six years old!

Whilst Margaret busied herself with bedding the three of us in to our new home and with Shân, now over four months old and beginning to be more aware of her surroundings, I commenced the first of twenty-four years working for Anglesey's new agricultural messiah, Morgan Evans.

The first task presented to me was to approve, and sign, the employment contract which Morgan's solicitors had prepared. I still have it, and it is amusing to read that one of its conditions was to prevent me, in the event of leaving the firm, from operating in the auction business anywhere on Anglesey for two years, should I depart for any reason. It was couched in quite long, legal jargon and was the identical type of restraint of trade clause which Bob Parry & Co. had threatened to invoke through the courts when Morgan decided to leave them! By today, such clauses are very difficult for employers to impose on a departing employee.

The Gospel According to Morgan Evans

No sooner had I spent my first day in the Llangefni office (this, and the livestock market in Gaerwen, were the only two operating bases) than Morgan called me into his 'den' for a welcoming chat.

We engaged in useful small talk before he declared, "I have only two very serious points that I want you to embrace from the very outset. My seventeen years whilst with Bob Parry & Co. have taught me the vital importance and value of the 'small' man. Anglesey has as many, if not more, smallholders than 'big' farmers and it is vital that all who come to work for me in the company, fully embrace that philosophy".

"Many of my customers are small farmers who may only produce forty cattle a year but who bring all those cattle to Gaerwen to sell. Then you have the 'big' farmer who produces perhaps one hundred and fifty cattle a year. He may bring sixty of those cattle to us, send forty to Bob Parry & Co. and the remaining fifty directly to the abattoir. The smallholder who chooses to bring all his output to us is therefore every bit as important as the bigger farmer who may bring us more cattle than the smallholder, but who chooses to spread his custom three ways".

I took this advice on board wholeheartedly and it is to his very great credit that Morgan continued embracing that philosophy just as enthusiastically, to my knowledge, twenty and more, years later. In pursuance of this commendable edict, it was common for all members of staff, including Morgan himself, to be seen on market days helping customers in all manner of ways – opening pen gates, herding animals into their pens and even to the extent of reversing the occasional clapped-out trailer into its correct position for unloading.

I remember one elderly customer with a well-worn Ford Cortina car and an even more well-worn trailer with two sheep as passengers, asking me earnestly in Welsh upon arrival in the yard – "*uw Rogars Jones, fasach chi mor garedig a bacio hon i'r lle iawn imi, fyddai ddim ond yn dreifio 'mlaen, byth yn ol*" (O, Rogers Jones, would you just be kind enough to back this into the right place for me, I normally only drive forwards, never in reverse!) It was this same philosophy of 'help everybody,' which had made Morgan so popular with the customers of Bob Parry & Co., during his time there.

He went on – "The second important point I wish to emphasise is this. Don't ever make the mistake of criticising anyone in the farming community here on Anglesey within earshot of another farmer or his family, because there is a more than an even chance that they will be related to one another!" Never was truer advice ever given, I was to realise on many occasions later in my career!

Finally, a welcome note of reassurance from Morgan: "I fully realise that your auction experience has, hitherto, been more or less restricted to the furniture and antiques side of the profession. Don't worry, we shall soon have you in that ring auctioning animals as well." At the time, this was truly reassuring, but at the same time, rather scary for someone rather vague as to the difference between a bull and a bullock and between a cow and a heifer!

Gaerwen Livestock Mart

1968 was coming to an end. Only about four years previously, Morgan had left Caernarfon to set up his own operation on Anglesey in opposition to the area's 'livestock market kings'. He had held his first auction of livestock in a paddock of a smallholding which he had acquired on a side lane at the back of Gaerwen Village.

It was an auction of the most basic type – on grass with

hurdles as temporary pens, but the customers turned up in good numbers to support this new messiah. Very soon the doubting Thomases, who previously had been laying bets as to how soon this crazy venture would fail, began to fall away and realise that this man Morgan Evans really did mean business.

Four years since its inception, as I was given a tour of the mart, now boasting a large area of hard-standing for vehicles, well-planned sheep pens with a weighing shed and a very impressive set of cattle penning, I began to marvel at how much had been achieved in such a comparatively short space of time. The cattle ring was the well-preserved building which had previously been the hay barn of the smallholding which Morgan had acquired. The mart 'office' was, for now at least, an old touring caravan and it was not very long before this became too small and very impractical for the increasing volume of business being generated.

Staffing numbers, in line with a well-managed new business, were small. The Llangefni estate and property office was expertly managed by Muriel Williams and that was about it up until my arrival. Morgan's right-hand man and market clerk was John Rees Thomas, an ex-Milk Marketing Board officer who was diligent and faithful and would have jumped through blazing hoops had he been ordered to by his boss. There were one or two market-day drovers and cleaners including the character of them all, William Roberts, or, as he was affectionately known to all, *'Wil Llain Big'* ... ...

'Wil Llain Big' (pronounced 'Beeg')
William Roberts hailed originally from a smallholding – Llain Big – in an Anglesey hamlet not far from Rhosneigr. He looked like what most of us would imagine an old-fashioned cattle drover to be like: small in stature, always

Wil Roberts (Llain Big) at work

Wil Roberts (Llain Big) at work

with a flat cap, ruddy complexion, thick, brown corduroy trousers and, on market days, gaiters and a pair of shiny boots.

Wil had worked for many years at a well-known farm, Cremlyn, Beaumaris, for the highly respected William Jones. I don't recall that he drove a vehicle; he relied on lifts to Gaerwen on sale days from locals who knew him well as a popular 'commuter' from his home in Llanddona, a village just northward of Beaumaris.

He was, should we say, fond of a tipple, one of his 'stopping-off' points after a day at the mart, being The Sailor's Return in Beaumaris. There were occasions when Wil was less aware of his surroundings during the second leg of his journey home than during the first!

He was responsible, along with others at the mart, for all the tasks associated with the safe penning of the animals and assisting farmers to load and unload etc. But the task he undoubtedly enjoyed most and for which he became so well known, was that of ringmaster on cattle auction days. He and his beloved boss, Morgan, had almost become a comic duo on sale days – the Boss efficient and serious, but with hidden humour, and Wil his puppet when an occasion demanded some light-hearted relief.

He always had a quiet, calm way with him in the ring – never the extravagant gesture which might frighten an animal and always with a consistent, measured pace as he strode the ring. But sometimes, a slightly excitable continental-bred animal would fall out of line and catch Wil unawares. Morgan would interrupt his selling flow and make a fully audible remark directed at Wil –"Hey, William Roberts, had a heavy time last night, did we?" and the assembled farmers would start chuckling.

Without hesitation and without altering his pace and as quick as a flash, Wil would reply, "Yes Mr Evans, quite heavy, but I can't give you the full details in front of all your customers"!

Wil would have a twinkle in his eye and a sly grin as he milked the appreciation of all the ringside customers!

I was to continue enjoying the company, hard graft and humour of '*Wil Llain Big*' for many more years and I feel certain that Morgan would fully endorse my view that he came out of a very special mould. He remained a faithful member of the Morgan Evans team until shortly before his death in 1981 at 81 years old.

About two years after my start with Morgan, he managed to prise away from Bob Parry & Co. another promising member of their team who, Morgan felt, would be just the person to join what had now become an increasingly vibrant and expanding operation. Maldwyn Williams had started his career in Caernarfon with Bob Parry & Co. on exactly the same day as I, way back in 1963.

I do not recall Maldwyn ever being given a nickname by our farming customers but if I had to give him two, they would be 'Mr Unflappable' and 'Mr Dependable,' and he remains, to this day, forty-five years on, the most experienced and vital cog in the company machine and respected by all who deal with him.

Irish Cattle

On a personal level, my confidence on the livestock rostrum was increasing with every sale. The actual selling part was no problem; in very basic terms, selling a sideboard and a four-legged beast require the same sort of technique. What I had to keep improving was my quick assessment of an animal in the very short time available between its entry into the sale ring and the commencement of the bidding.

The technique required an immediate 'visual x-ray' of the beast along its whole length in the space of a few seconds. Spotting bids was the other task; taking bids in a furniture saleroom is usually quite easy, bidders are expected to indicate their intentions by showing their bidding cards. No such thing happens in a livestock auction. Indeed, you can be staring at a farmer or dealer directly into his face and as close as you might be to him, you may still not be able to spot his bidding technique. A slight raise of one eyebrow, a movement of the upper lip or the bending of the top joint of one little finger, are but simple examples of the bidding methods used.

One of my favourite exponents of the 'invisible bid' was lovely Jackie Rowlands, a well-known dealer-farmer from Llanddeusant. You had to be looking at Jackie's eyelashes, never mind at his eyebrows, to be able to have any chance of detecting his bidding technique!

Anglesey's non-prime agricultural land had long been a favourite for the finishing of well-boned Irish cattle. When Morgan was approached by a respected dealer from over the water to conduct Irish cattle sales on his behalf, he immediately jumped at the opportunity which he quite understandably saw as a handy means of increasing

A busy Friday at Gaerwen – Maldwyn Williams and the late Meic Pari giving a helping hand.

company turnover.

The cattle came over from Dublin Port in special compartments on a ferry and would then complete the journey from Holyhead to Gaerwen via conventional livestock wagons. On arrival at the mart, the beasts would be sorted into lots by the dealer; I recall that lots of between six and twelve would be fairly typical and that such lotting was intended to cater for all pockets.

The auction would commence in its customary way and one or two lots might, (or, as was most often the case, might not,) be sold. This was the point at which the auction as we know it, ended, and marked the beginning of what we all regarded as the most boring, long-winded part of the whole operation.

As most of us are aware, our good friends from the Emerald Isle are the absolute past masters at the 'talk-talk' and the horse (or 'cattle' in this case) trading. They just all love the bartering and the brinkmanship at which they are the real experts. So after the 'auction' in the ring, the 'real sale', at least in the eyes of the dealer, would take place on a one-to-one level down in the sale yard.

But this was why we all saw it as the most boring of events – it would usually take the whole of the remainder of that day. We had to just hang around waiting for hands to be shaken, denoting that a deal had been agreed. It was not at all uncommon for one of our customers to commence negotiations in the morning to buy a bunch of cattle he very much fancied, only for negotiations to break down and for the farmer to go home for his lunch and return in the afternoon to recommence battle! But our Irish friends just loved a system which they had been brought up on and one which they generally knew would see them coming out on top. The company got its sale commission in the usual way, but a time and motion expert would have had a field day on discovering how long it sometimes took to sell eighty or so Irish cattle. Never mind that the mart was simply used as a convenient bartering venue for our friends from across the water!

Receipts and Billheads
I confess to being a long-time sufferer of an incurable affliction. I think the medical name for it is Nostalgiaitis, for which there is no known cure.

It all started one afternoon when I visited a farming client at Llangaffo, a short distance from the mart in Gaerwen. Mr Evans of Bodowyr Isaf was a lovely man, an ordinary farmer of quiet disposition who was a faithful customer at the mart.

As I was driving along the lane leading to the farm, I came across Mr Evans standing guard over a well-established bonfire. I wound the window down and, in Welsh, expressed the hope that there "were no £10 notes in there". He replied that he was getting rid of a huge pile of old receipts, a task he'd been meaning to carry out for a long time.

Having, as I did at the time, one or two personal old family receipts at home, I immediately enquired of Mr Evans if there were any left which had not succumbed to his blazing pile, whereupon I was invited to have a good rummage and help myself.

My rummaging revealed one or two gems which I cherish to this day. The lovely thing about old receipts is that, almost without fail, they give us a graphic illustration of how business in pre-computer days in the early part of the century was conducted; the polite, almost genteel, way of doing things and, in so many instances, the total reliance which the rural populace placed on the local store or post office. Hence the oft-used Welsh term *'Siop Pob Dim'*, literally translated as 'The Everything Shop'.

One of Mr Evans' receipts which typically illustrates the function then of the local village store is from the 'Post Office and Steam Bakery' run by W Thomas & Sons of Llangaffo, located just a stone's throw from Bodowyr Isaf. The billhead reads 'Drapers, Outfitters, Family Grocers, Ironmongers, Flour and Corn Dealers, Coal Merchants etc.' Phew!

The receipted bill is written in pencil and covers, astonishingly, a 10-month period during 1922 and 1924. The word 'cashflow' had evidently not been invented in those days! Here is an example of the diverse nature of the purchases on this one receipt: 'Pint Mug, Cord Trousers, Bun Loaf, Cycle Tyre, Chick Food and a Meat Dish' and, together with one or two other items, the whole lot came to £4/18s.

Soon after my Bodowyr bonanza, I made a call to a traditional Anglesey worker's cottage at Llanerchymedd. The property was quite sparsely furnished but did contain a pleasing quantity of traditional oak items. There was a dresser, a chest of drawers, a set of four oak chairs, a round table, a settle and a dressing table. All quite ordinary items but very saleable in, what was at the time, quite a buoyant market. I gave the client my opinion that, on a good day, all the contents would realise between £2,000 and £3,000.

She seemed happy with my forecast, and so the paperwork was prepared and arrangements made to collect the items via one of our carriers. With small talk finished and the usual thanks given, I made my way to the front door of the cottage, whereupon the lady client suddenly exclaimed, "I completely forgot to mention, I have the original receipt for the making of all the items which you have listed today". I did a double take and stared at her both in disbelief and anticipation at such a revelation.

The receipt, in the name of '*Hugh M Jones (Late of Liverpool), Builder and Contractor*' was dated July 19th 1898 and listed all the items seen by me in the cottage, except for '2 Beds' which must have long since disappeared. The total cost was £20 17s 6d. Oh, and that included 3s 6d in respect of 'tongued and grooved boards and battens and nails'.

Sadly, the client was not prepared to release the receipt with the furniture but she did allow me to make photocopies, one of which is now a cherished item in my collection.

In 1877, my great-grandfather, a builder and joiner in the village of Cynwyd, a traditional Clwydian village just up the road from Corwen, built the Baptist chapel. I have in my proud possession the original eight-line estimate, hand written in ink on a small, random piece of paper and it reads: 'I John Nathaniel Edwards of Bryntrystion, Cynwyd do hereby agree to contract for the New Baptist Chapel at Cynwyd and to complete the same according to the plans and specifications in a Workmanlike manner for the sum of

Four Hundred and Seventy Five Pounds.' Not even a formal address, from or to, on the bit of paper, almost as if it had been written down over a chat and a cup of tea.

Far more formal, but a great accompaniment to the main receipt, is one from the Great Western Railway for the transport of 2,000 bricks from Trevor to Cynwyd on August 30th 1877, for the grand sum of 'One Pound.' It took me some while to reconcile the use of 2,000 bricks in a stone-built chapel until I paid a visit to Cynwyd and realised that they were for the lintels and wall angles.

Sadly, the word at the commencement of 2013 was that my great-grandfather's dear little chapel was to become yet another one under threat of closure.

Due to the kindness of fellow Nostalgiaitis sufferers in the Llanrwst area, I have several receipts relating to businesses there which include some for the auction company Robert and Rogers Jones. It is wrongly assumed by many, that there is a family connection, but no, it is just one of those coincidences. I have a receipt for the sale of a mare by auction in 1929 for what appears to be the huge sum at that time of fifty-nine guineas, and one which doubtless reflects the importance of the horse in those far-off days.

I also have a fine and colourful 'mini-poster' by Robert and Rogers Jones advertising a *Great Annual Sale* at *Dyffryn Mymbyr* on behalf of the famous Thomas Firbank – *'1,300 Grand Hill Sheep and 29 Welsh and Crossbred Cattle at Llanrwst Smithfield on Saturday, September 16, 1939'*. If you wanted to telephone the auctioneers concerning the sale, the number to ring was '15' Llanrwst!

The reader may well regard me as a rather sad old figure indulging in such nostalgic bits of paper but I do feel that in today's computer-led, materialistic society, they definitely have a place, especially on those winter evenings when the

By direction of Thomas Firbank, Esq.

Dyffryn Mymbyr – Great Annual Sale

Of upwards of

1,300 GRAND HILL SHEEP

Comprising

700 STRONG HEALTHY EWES
200 CHOICE EWE LAMBS
400 Forward WETHER LAMBS
SEVERAL STOCK RAMS

Also

29 WELSH and CROSSBRED CATTLE

Comprising

Bulling Heifers and Strong Wintering Bullocks
PROMISING CART FILLY FOAL

100 R.I.R. (1938) PULLETS.   100 Cross R.I.R. and
Light Sussex PULLETS (5 months old).

———

To be Sold by Public Auction at the

LLANRWST SMITHFIELD

Where the stock will be moved for the convenience of purchasers, on

SATURDAY, SEPTEMBER 16, 1939,

AT 12-30 O'CLOCK.

USUAL CREDIT TERMS.

ROBERT & ROGERS JONES, F.A.I.,

AUCTIONEERS.

Ty'n-y-Fynwent, Llanrwst.   Telephone: 15 Llanrwst.

T. S. Harrison, Printing Office, 30 Denbigh Street, Llanrwst.

Copy of a poster for an auction at the farm of Thomas Firbank in Capel Curig (the author has no connection with this auction company).

offerings on the 'telly' are somewhat on the thin side.

Technology Early 1970s
By the early 1970s, I had become reasonably confident and proficient in the sale of both beef and store cattle. Whichever of us was not, at a particular moment, actually selling, would do the clerking work on the rostrum. I used to enjoy this aspect of rostrum work as much as the selling itself. It gave one the opportunity to study the bidding techniques of the buyers and to enjoy a ringside view, as it were, of the occasional humorous interludes which took place.

Store cattle are sold by auction in any number or numbers determined by the owner. A typical bunch of stores might be anything between six and twelve. However, beef cattle are sold singly with each beast weighed on a 'walk-on' machine before entering the salering.

Two distinct elements made up the hammer price – the weight of the animal in hundredweights to the nearest half and quarter, and the price per hundredweight as bid by the buyer. Now, if one imagines each beast on a good day taking no more than about thirty seconds to be sold, from the time it entered the ring to the hammer falling, the person clerking the sale would need to be very much on his or her toes in order to keep up with proceedings.

Assisting the clerk in this operation would be a 'cattle ready reckoner' in book form, the pages of which would be flipped, as soon as the animal was weighed, to the page containing the particular weight of the beast. Immediately the hammer price was declared, the clerk's eyes would need to speedily scan down the page to the point where weight and price columns met to give the overall selling price. This, together with the buyer's name would then be hand recorded on 'sale sheets' to then be processed by clerical staff in the mart office (or caravan).

On one fine day, which I shall always remember, this archaic, (as it appears in retrospect), system of calculating prices came to an end quite abruptly.

A good customer of the firm and one who always tended to be the forerunner when any new innovations came on the market (he owned a Leica camera, of which everyone was envious) marched into the office one day and proudly declared, with suitable wide smile, "Look what I've got, boys", and what we all found ourselves staring at was, for heaven's sake, a pocket calculator made by Texas Instruments which he'd bought for the enormous price of £375! We all looked at this revolutionary new thing in some disbelief and with great envy, but it really was not all that long before our beloved green-bound ready reckoners were consigned to the ready reckoner pit in the sky, never to see the light of day ever again!

Mobile Phones

I had cause, one fine morning, to pay a visit to Holyhead on a property-related matter, a building society valuation, I think. In the seventies, the new 'A55 super highway' was but a far-off dream, so a visit to Holyhead, or indeed to any other part of the north of the island, usually entailed a rather more sedate journey along one of two highways which dissected Anglesey.

I duly carried out what was required of me in Holyhead and returned to the office in Llangefni, some two hours later. My anger was very pronounced and the air somewhat blue on being told by the office that very urgent instructions had been received from solicitors for me to carry out a valuation that afternoon if at all possible – in Holyhead!

In a very bad-tempered mood, and with much door-banging, I returned to my trusty Vauxhall Cavalier, in order to make the required repeat journey to Holyhead. It was during this second trip that I determined, there and then, to acquire a car phone so that such a comical, time-wasting scenario did not occur again. Now a car phone in those days, meant exactly what it said on the label – a telephone for use within the confines of the motor car. The word 'mobile' did not come into it at that early stage. And the innovator of this type of high-tech device was – Motorola.

The first mobile telephone call was, apparently, made on 3rd April, 1973, with Motorola apparatus so big and cumbersome, potential users might have thought that they were handling one of those heavy-duty, instant start battery chargers which garages use to get stranded motorists on their way. You apparently had half an hour of calls before the beast required recharging; but, never mind, it was soon seen as the start of something big and we all know the rest of the story.

An appointment was duly made with our local garage for the Vauxhall to be there for a whole day for the aerial and wiring for the car telephone to be installed. I picked up the car on completion of the installation together with the all-important handset which looked, and felt like, a cross between a truncheon and an elongated, slightly bent, banana. It was secured within the car by a bracket and it was virtually impossible to commit the modern offence of 'using the phone whilst driving', as it would have been too heavy!

Most importantly, however, it did the trick and served the intended purpose of avoiding time-wasting, repeat journeys along the narrow roads of Anglesey. Very soon, of course, the in-car telephone became a very sophisticated business tool, only for itself to be superseded by better and better equipment until, before very long the Apples, the Blackberries, the Nokias and the Samsungs et al, all came along to delight us, or to make our lives a misery, depending on our particular point of view.

Murder Most Foul (1)

On the 4th of March 1969, a Mrs Sarah Hughes of Valley, Anglesey was brutally murdered.

Two days later, a telephone call was received at the office from the Gwynedd Constabulary asking if two detectives on the case could come over forthwith in order to 'eliminate David Rogers Jones from their enquiries'. Mrs Hughes was a client of the firm, as the landlady of property in Holyhead, which we used to manage on her behalf. Two days prior to her untimely death, I had paid a visit to her bungalow home near Four Mile Bridge to discuss, at her request, various matters. An extremely vigilant neighbour had spotted my dark blue Morris 1100 estate car outside Mrs Hughes' property and reported accordingly to the police.

I was duly eliminated from police enquiries, but the person who was not, turned out to be a 14-year old local boy who, on ransacking the bungalow and stealing £10, stabbed Mrs Hughes repeatedly with a knife. He was convicted of murder and released from prison after seven years, only to be found guilty again in 1986 of a second murder, that of a Cumbrian lady hotel owner, for which he was sentenced to life imprisonment with no recommendation as to the minimum time to be served.

Antiques for Sale

By 1973 two boys had arrived as brothers for Shân and as the bread-winner for five of us I was now conscious of the need to try and assert my position as chattels auctioneer within the company.

The time had now come for me to seriously attempt to exploit the possibilities of commencing regular auctions of antiques, fine art and the like at the mart where the customer base was increasing at a very encouraging pace. This was, after all, primarily what I had been trained to do. With the mart complex still in its comparatively raw infancy, so far as covered livestock accommodation was concerned, the possibilities were fairly limited.

Fortunately, our hands were forced on the issue, when we received instructions from Caernarfon solicitors to empty the contents of a bungalow in the town which had recently been the victim of quite a severe accidental fire. Whilst the property itself had suffered very badly, the very nice antiques had not, except for the not-insignificant effect of smoke, which had stained every single thing and which was obvious even to the most undiscerning of nostrils.

'Plan A' was the only plan we had, so it was decided that this inaugural auction of antiques would be held in the cattle ring, with use being made of the quite spacious covered side areas which were normally used for the assembly and sorting of cattle before they entered the sale ring.

Now the only major snag was that the store cattle auctions took place on a Tuesday and the fat cattle on the following Friday – every week, all year round. In between those two days therefore, the ring and all the adjoining areas had to be comprehensively and very thoroughly washed down prior to the delivery of antiques and furniture.

This all had to take place on the Wednesday, for the lotting to be carried out prior to the auction itself on the Thursday. I have to confess that there were many subsequent occasions when items for an antique auction were being brought into a still soaking-wet sale ring, following its hosepipe treatment. There was always the fear that every bit of cattle muck might not have been washed away, as it would have been unthinkable for a Mrs Hughes' or a Mrs Roberts' Burberry raincoat to suffer the very obvious embarrassment occasioned by lurking cattle muck!

This was not the only practical problem; the floor of a cattle ring is slightly domed and ridged for grip and cleaning purposes which was not particularly conducive to the stability of tables containing potentially valuable artefacts.

Despite having to make an attempt at cleaning the smoke-affected Caernarfon items (not to be recommended too often), this first auction went very well, as I recall, and was to be the forerunner of many, many more in this slightly unconventional location.

What was so funny to behold was that in place of the usual crowd of flat-capped farmers in wellingtons, we had the well-dressed wives of those farmers with their baskets, their knitting and a copy of '*Yr Herald Mon*' (the local 'rag') with the occasional 'best dresseds' sitting in a tiered, wooden-seated cattle ring usually reserved for cattle, and not for antique, dealers. Many of our 'old' customers still refer nostalgically and affectionately to those days as being much less 'clinical' than the general atmosphere in today's auction salerooms.

A new purpose-built saleroom was built in the mart complex in 1976 by the Crendon Concrete Company and was to prove a landmark development in the fortunes of the firm. Almost forty years on, auctions are still being conducted there.

Auctions – Getting it Right

Property auctions in a mixed agricultural and residential practice are always an important facet of any business. Morgan Evans & Company was no exception.

Whilst it may well sound boastful, my success record for property auctions, both agricultural and residential, during my twenty-four years in the company, was very high, but such a statistic did not concern me sufficiently to make a note of it. The secret, if that is the right word, of such success is very simple and not, as they say, rocket science. You simply do not take on a property for auction unless you are pretty certain that the result will be a sale.

As I stated earlier, the word 'public' is exactly what it says; the whole world will hear of a successful outcome whilst an unsuccessful outcome will be even more talked about. It always surprised me how often I was approached by owners to place their property on the market by auction, they having struggled without any success to secure a buyer by private treaty. The maxim always is that 'an auction does not, of itself, create the customer, the customers have to be there already, an auction simply being the means of bringing that competition to the public domain'. I have never wavered from that view.

Early on in my property auctioning career, I was to learn a very valuable lesson. The process of placing a property, be it a residential, commercial or agricultural property, on the market for sale was basically identical regardless of how the property was going to be marketed. After the initial inspection, sale details would be prepared and, where appropriate, plans outlining the extent of the property, particularly in the case of agricultural land would be drawn up, approved, and finalised.

The huge difference here in the UK, excepting possibly Scotland, between an auction and a private treaty sale is that the purchaser at auction pays a 10 per cent deposit on the hammer price and signs a contract there and then.

I had received instructions from executors to offer by auction a medium-sized farm in quite a remote part of Anglesey and which comprised good land, reasonable outbuildings but with a semi-derelict, unoccupied farmhouse.

Plenty of neighbouring and far-off farmers had lined themselves up as potential buyers so that, on the due auction day at our premises in Llangefni, I was very confident indeed of a successful outcome. The usual auction procedures were followed; an introduction by me, the auctioneer, then the conditions of sale read out by the acting solicitor, before my again asking if there were any final questions or queries before asking for bids.

At this juncture, a well-dressed gentleman of good bearing rose out of his chair at the back of the room to ask if he could be informed as to who was to be responsible for the reconstruction of approximately thirty-five metres of dressed stone walling between the council highway and one of the farm's fields. A surprising and most unwelcome question indeed. I stared firstly at the assembled crowd, then at the solicitor, who, in turn stared back at me with a very pleading look, obviously praying for an answer to this awkward and potentially embarrassing, query.

I suddenly realised that the instigator of this enquiry knew precisely the circumstances surrounding the damaged wall, having carefully done his homework properly, which was more than could be said of me. It transpired that a milk tanker of the very large variety had overshot the road verge, lost control and had promptly come to rest many yards down the road with dressed stone scattered all over the place.

Neither we, nor the solicitors, had been informed of this rather dramatic change to the character of such a length of stone walling. In the absence of an owner in the saleroom to consult, the solicitor immediately assured the assembled throng that the responsibility for both the repair and cost of the wall would be that of the sellers of the farm.

Everyone felt suitably reassured and the auction continued without further hitch; unfortunately, the gentleman who had raised the problem of the wall initially, ended up losing out against two other very strong bidders.

The lesson to be learnt here, of course, was that the slightest or biggest physical change can happen to any property at a moment's notice without any warning. Every single property auction which I conducted thereafter was preceded by a final physical inspection not more than twenty-four hours prior to the time of the auction. I became particularly diligent thereafter where stone walls were concerned!

Charles Williams

Countless numbers of Welsh people still mourn the passing of the Anglesey actor, raconteur and comedian known affectionately by all as Charles. Whenever the name was mentioned in Welsh broadcasting, television or '*noson lawen*' circles, everyone knew to whom the name of Charles referred.

His talents, (and they were true talents, unlike the so-called talents of many of today's overpaid, sometimes controversial stars), were absolutely multi-various. It was his natural, in-bred talent for saying something quite hilarious in the course of a seemingly innocuous conversation which reminds me of an encounter I had with him one morning in Llangefni.

Charles hailed from the sleepy village of Bodffordd, a couple of miles or so from Anglesey's market town. Instantly recognisable wherever he went, not for Charles the pretensions of a flash motor car, only, as I recall, a fairly aged Japanese thing which had no doubt bumped its way along Anglesey lanes for many thousands of hilarious miles.

I had occasion one morning to step out of the office, only to be confronted by this easily recognisable Japanese car parked on the yellow lines near the office entrance. As I came out, a window wound down to release the lovely, gravelly drawl of Charles Williams. "*Uw, Rogers Jones, jest y dyn 'dwisho weld, dowch i mewn i'r car 'ma am funud bach ini gael sgwrs*" (Hey, Rogers Jones, just the man I want to see, pop into the car for a moment for a chat).

I dutifully eased myself into the passenger seat, knowing full well that on exiting that vehicle my day will have been enriched by some witty snippet or other delivered in Charles' own inimitable way.

"I tell you what I've got in mind. I have a house in Bodffordd which I'm thinking of selling."

Immediately I realised that this was potentially serious office business and that there would be no frivolity or joking during the course of this impromptu roadside discussion. He continued. "It's in the village centre, just off the Square, terraced, two up, two down, really quite small and the time has come, I think, to get rid of it. It's in quite poor condition really. I should think a damn good fart would have it down in no time at all"!

Now in Charles' small Japanese runabout there really was not a lot of room in which to fall about laughing, but fall about I did, only for Charles to turn slowly and quizzically towards me as if to ask, "Was it something I said?" If ever confirmation were needed of Charles Williams' natural humour as well as his rehearsed and practiced humour, then this was surely it. My whole day was duly fulfilled and I would be guaranteed to 'milk' the delightful anecdote for some time to come!

Waiting for Ercol

There will be few, if any, Anglesey people, particularly those from Llangefni and its environs, who will not be familiar with '*Siop DC*' the highly respected and long-established house furnishing shop in the centre of the town.

The business was founded by DC Williams in 1956 and has flourished very successfully to this day. DC's enduring success was the result of his insistence on selling quality goods, and the very personable and 'smooth' way he dealt with his customers, not only from the island but also from much further afield. His trading philosophy ensured much repeat business from his very many farming customers. Sadly, DC passed away in 2008, but the excellent business philosophy which he pursued has been continued by his son, Michael, to this day.

One day, sometime in the 80s, I had cause to visit the shop for some relatively mundane reason. A well-dressed, beaming lady from the farming community whom I knew, exited DC's shop just as I entered. She had gone in to purchase a lightwood Ercol dresser and was happy with what she had been shown in the catalogue. DC went into the office to enquire of Ercol on the phone, how long delivery of the dresser would take. On being given a 3-month order date, DC feared that he would lose the deal. He need not have worried; it was just the news she wanted to hear. She could tell all her friends that her brand new Ercol dresser was going to take 'nearly three months to arrive,' such was the high quality of the furniture she had ordered.

Now, coincidentally, shortly afterwards, DC received a highly coveted invitation to an expenses-paid visit to the Ercol Factory in High Wycombe, Buckinghamshire. He must have been a good retailer of Ercol goods to have received such an invite.

Many people may not realise that the Ercol furniture business dates back as far as 1920, having been founded by Lucian Ercolani, who died in 1976. The quality of production is still second to none today, and the demand for its models very high despite the quite 'tasty' prices.

DC was enjoying his tour of the factory and in particular talking to long-serving craftsmen and their sons who had been at the Factory for years and years. He was taken into a gigantic, hangar-like warehouse where, to his great surprise, there were rows upon rows of lightwood Ercol dressers!

Now having recently submitted the order for his Anglesey customer and been given such a long delivery date, DC was, understandably, somewhat puzzled by this sight of so many lovely dressers.

His immediate reaction was to gently ask his guide the reason for such a long delivery date when there appeared to be a very plentiful supply of the items.

With a lovely wink in his eye, the guide slowly revealed the simple Ercol ethos to DC – "We never give our retailers an immediate delivery date, regardless of how many examples there may happen to be in stock. By giving an extended delivery date, you are guaranteed to be giving the customer that special feel of exclusivity which would otherwise be absent."

Ercol! Not only good furniture makers but also good business psychologists too.

I recall Michael Williams himself relating one of many anecdotes concerning his late father. D C had sold a new bed to an Anglesey vicar and his wife who had been good customers for many years. On the receipt which accompanied the delivery of the bed, D C had impishly added to the 'received with thanks' part, "I don't suppose you will get as much enjoyment from this one as you did the previous...."!

The sporting minded vicar, when next he came across D C, shook his fists at his bed retailer in mock anger. But he did have a broad smile on his face.

Your Set or Mine?

Wil was a big-time farmer from Llyn in south Caernarfonshire. He had just performed a neighbourly favour for an elderly brother and sister who owned a nearby smallholding, in return for which they invited Wil to 'swper' (supper) one evening by way of a thank you.

On arrival at the smallholding, it was evident to the guest that a lot of trouble had gone into providing a worthy feast. After some soup, the main course of roast beef was brought in whereupon the brother and sister, and their guest Wil, proceeded to tuck into the lovely fare.

Wil quietly tackled the delicious roast beef and as he was contemplating which might be the local source of such good meat, the brother suddenly exclaimed, "This beef is really rather tough today," which came as rather a surprise to the guest who carried on eating as if nothing had been said. A further surprise came when the sister also exclaimed that her beef was also "very tough". Suddenly, and without any preamble, the brother put down his knife and fork and deftly stuffed a crinkled, brown hand into his mouth to extract a fairly fine set of dentures, holding them up for his sister to see. This was the signal for her to do exactly the same, by which time Wil was not quite sure where to put himself.

Brother and sister proceeded to carry out a sort of visual inspection of the gnashers across the table and without a single word between them, the dentures were exchanged and expertly installed in the correct respective mouths, with both of them exclaiming, almost as one, "That's better, nothing at all wrong with the beef after all"!

Wil had no option but to carry on eating just as if nothing at all had happened!

Olympic Heroine (1)

I received a call one morning to visit two sisters who lived in a converted windmill near Trearddur Bay. I duly went along to fulfil what I assumed was going to be a routine call, one of many which I would have carried out by the end of the working week. I was introduced to two very delicate-looking elderly ladies of striking elegance and poise; one of the sisters seemed to be in good physical shape but it was immediately apparent that the other was very badly affected by arthritis, judging by her distressingly knurled fingers and her profuse apologies for not getting up due to her very painful difficulties with walking.

I soon concluded the business which they had called me in to discuss, whereupon we got down to a bit of the usual 'small talk' which I have always enjoyed and felt to be very much part of getting to know customers I am meeting for the very first time. The diverse interest and backgrounds of clients from all walks of life will always give an intense glow of satisfaction and the meeting with these two charming ladies was to be no exception.

Out of the blue and almost at a complete tangent in the conversation, the arthritic sister very casually and without drama nor a hint of boasting, declared that she "had skated for Great Britain in the 1936 Berlin Olympic Games" and, almost as an aside, declared: "I came in third". I looked amazed at both of the sisters, conscious that I was perhaps staring rather too intently at the terribly bent and misshapen hands as I tried to equate her achievement all those years ago with the sad looking figure sitting in front of me.

She went on to say that as a young lady, hitherto fairly shielded from the troubles of the outside world, it was the first time that she had been outside the United Kingdom and the journey to Berlin had been by train, courtesy of a third class rail ticket provided by her particular athletics organisation.

What a far-off cry from today's elite training programmes, kit sponsorship, flashy product advertising promotions and media exposure which today's athletes seem to require! But I don't think for one moment that this wonderful, unassuming and disarmingly modest lady would have, for a single second, resented the incredible changes since the far-off days of those infamous Berlin Olympic Games.

Jack Griffiths

I only wish that I could remember more about Jack Griffiths, but one anecdote concerning him will last me for ever. Jack was a smallholder from somewhere in the middle of Anglesey. Amongst his more well-known attributes was that of sometime bare-knuckle fighter at '*Ffair Borth*,' the annual autumnal fair at Menai Bridge where, prior to 'Health and Safety' and a myriad of other regulations, the public could try its hand at many rural, and sometimes not quite so rural, competitive practices. Jack had a wonderful, always-smiling disposition and, in accordance with his past experiences was very much the showman with an engaging swagger about him.

For precise reasons which I cannot recall, Jack gave the company instructions to conduct a dispersal sale at his smallholding on the island. It was held on a Saturday afternoon as I recall and, as with all farm dispersal sales, Jack's immediate farming neighbours as well as others came to support him from all parts of the island.

Anglesey's farmers were second to none when it came to supporting such an event. You would have to have been a really unpopular sort not to be afforded the degree of loyalty being shown to Jack on this particular afternoon. The chance of a bargain or two was also no less a reason for making an appearance at a dispersal sale, particularly as a buyer would know the precise source and genuine nature of all the items on offer.

The sale commenced with a few cattle and sheep and some poultry and a pig or two and ended with the machinery such as it was. There were a few elderly, but quite serviceable bits of machinery on offer, before the time came to put up for sale Jack's *piece de resistance*, his trusty tractor and muck spreader, probably the two most valuable assets in the auction.

Already Jack had shown during the proceedings his engaging tendencies towards showmanship; he would make a bit of a meal out of a shovel and rake if he thought it would raise a chuckle with the crowd. So it was no surprise to any one of us when he declared to Morgan, who was conducting the auction that "he was going to give a bit of a demo of his Fordson tractor and Massey Ferguson muck-spreader before the bidding commenced".

Morgan, in his politest but most authoritative and persuasive way, in order to save time apart from anything else, politely declined the suggestion, telling the beaming and enthusiastic Jack Griffiths that "there really was no need as the customers could see for themselves what they were – excellent in every respect." But it became obvious that Jack was having none of it, despite Morgan's further efforts at dissuasion. He had planned to be the leading player in this part of the proceedings and was not going to have his moment denied, even by Morgan Evans himself.

The machinery was all assembled tidily at the bottom of a gently sloping paddock, with all the customers and Morgan and me lined up along the bottom of the paddock. On realising Jack's serious demonstrating intentions, the farmers all began chatting and speculating as to how exactly it was all going to end up, knowing Jack as they did and knowing, more importantly, that this was likely to be an 'anything could happen situation'.

Jack leapt into the tractor cab, got the Fordson started with a huge cloud of fumes and proceeded to take an anti-clockwise loop up the slope of the paddock. It was quite a slow haul up that hill, particularly as Jack had seen fit to load the spreader to the top with the wettest and smelliest muck he could lay his shovels on.

Jack eventually reached the highest part of the field at which point it became time to activate the muck spreader.

Now for those unfamiliar with 'manurial machinations', a word or two of explanation. Unlike the relatively sophisticated, cylinder-shaped spreaders of today (this was, after all, the 1970s), Jack's spreader was, to all intents and purposes, an open truck with two rear wheels and a hitch to the tractor and containing a large, corkscrew-like steel worm which, on being activated by the tractor driver, would rotate through the muck and spread it reasonably evenly over the land. That was the general idea.

Easy so far, except for one vitally important thing – the muck is intended, and I emphasise the word 'intended', to exit from the spreader rearwards, yes, rearwards. Immediately after Jack was seen by us all to activate the handle, it became obvious to all that there was one vital thing wrong. The muck had started exiting in vast, smelly quantities in a forward, rather than a rearward, direction.

Now Jack's trusty Fordson tractor did, at least, enjoy the luxury of a cab. The only slight, or rather major, snag in this case was that the cab did not have a panel at the rear, which would have given poor Jack the luxury of some protection from the vast quantities of brown stuff coming his way.

By now, the spectating customers, on realising what was happening at the top of this field, began to fall about laughing uncontrollably whilst Jack, ever the showman, continued his drive back down the field just as if nothing untoward had taken place.

He stopped the tractor near us, jumped down out of the cab, completely covered in best-quality Anglesey manure, as was the tractor itself – and gave us all a huge, white-toothed grin just as if there was nothing at all out of place.

The usually reverential Morgan Evans just could not contain himself and it was several minutes before we were all sufficiently composed to place these two objects of such entertainment under the hammer!

Electric Mountain

The name Mc Alpine Brand Zschokke may be totally forgotten by many local North Wales people by today. For others, however, the name, abbreviated to MBZ, will evoke memories of a prosperous era in the 1970s when hundreds of workers of all skills were engaged in the construction of the Dinorwig Hydro-Electric scheme, more commonly known today as Electric Mountain. Such was the importance and uniqueness of the scheme that it was always sufficient for all the workers to refer to their workplace just as 'MBZ', no other reference being necessary.

This consortium of three of the finest British and European companies, all specialists in their respective fields, commenced the gigantic operation of constructing, in very simple terms, an electric power station deep inside the bowels of one of Snowdonia's mountains in 1974.

The scheme took ten years to complete at a cost of £425 million and involved the removal of twelve million tons of rock from deep within the slate-covered Elidir Fawr mountain, overlooking Llanberis.

The question may be asked: what had this gigantic scheme got to do with auctioning and Morgan Evans & Co? As various parts of the operation were completed, so constructional machinery and plant became redundant, and required disposal in order to create space for the next, and subsequent, phases of the operation. About four public auctions were organised towards the late 70s and we were most pleased to be instructed to organise two of them. The plant and machinery were assembled for sale on site in and around Llanberis, where there were ample facilities and space for both the plant and parking of customers' vehicles.

Whilst I confidently took on the role of organiser and auctioneer (I was, by now, selling the machinery in many of our farm dispersal auctions), I did feel just a small degree of trepidation with the impending MBZ auction. These were not ordinary farm tractors and bucket diggers seen on a daily basis, but the rather more sophisticated collection of very heavy-duty plant which a contract of this magnitude would have required. One member of the construction consortia was, after all, foremost in Europe in the field of civil engineering tunnelling, so the plant and machinery would not have been of the Dinky Toy variety.

On both auction days, the customer response was terrific and the free budgetary hand which we had more or less been allowed in the promotion of the sale helped greatly too. My major concern right until the last minute, however, was whether, here, in 'semi-remote' North Wales, there were going to be the customers for such a wide range of specialist, heavy duty machinery.

I did not need to worry at all. The 1970s had seen quite an upsurge in demand from the Middle East for plant and machinery of the very type on offer in Llanberis. Major UK plant dealers had done their homework very thoroughly and had, in many cases, secured buyers for many of the items even before the auctions had taken place. We must have pleased our principals at the first auction sufficiently to be shown favour for a second auction a year or two later.

I have often wondered how much construction work in places like Dubai has taken place over the years with the assistance of plant and machinery which started its life tunnelling mountains in Llanberis, North Wales!

Charles Frederick Tunnicliffe

By the end of the 1980s, the new, purpose-built saleroom in Gaerwen, with all its excellent parking and loading facilities, was well and truly up and running, with memories of mucky pens and wet sale rings very much a thing of the past.

In 1979, the renowned bird artist and illustrator, C F

Tunnicliffe died. He had spent most of his productive life on his beloved Anglesey, which had been so inspirational for him and which had provided so many subjects for his work right on his doorstep.

Two years after his death, the whole of Charles Tunnicliffe's work was scheduled to be put up for sale by auction in London. It would therefore be split up and scattered wide, never again to be seen as a lifetime's collection to be enjoyed and studied by future generations.

The Ynys Mon (Anglesey) County Council, to its great credit, immediately set wheels in motion to try and secure the collection for Anglesey. Time was not on its side but it still had one good thing to come out of a certain pipeline buried deep under the island's farmland.

The Shell Oil Fund was a most valuable income stream arising from a very lengthy pipeline deep underground which transferred oil from Rhosgoch in the north of the island to Stanlow refinery near the Wirral. Some of the then, largest oil tankers in the world would berth off Amlwch for the valuable liquid cargo to be piped underwater to Rhosgoch and thereon over the mainland via the lower slopes of the Carneddau mountains to Stanlow Refinery.

The Anglesey County council to its credit saw the fund as an ideal means to facilitate the purchase of the Tunnicliffe collection for Anglesey. It acquired the collection in its entirety prior to the proposed auction, no doubt to the great disappointment of the appointed auctioneers. I know just how they must have hurt!

There then followed the enormous and painstaking task of preserving such an enormous collection of works, many of which were showing obvious signs of the effects of poor storage and the artist's use of materials not really intended for long endurance.

Fairly soon afterwards in 1985, Morgan Evans & Co.

were favoured with instructions from the Estate of Tunnicliffe's niece, Mrs Margaret (Peggy) Walker, to offer 120 lots of various works by the artist. This was a marvellous auction for us to hold so soon after all the publicity pertaining to Anglesey's acquisition of the main collection.

It also proved a good opportunity to capitalise as soon as possible on that publicity, to which end I organised two further auctions of Tunnicliffe's work in May and October 1986 totalling nearly 600 varied works by the artist, including rare books which had been illustrated by him.

Some of these lots came directly from the artist's Cheshire family but outside sources were also good contributors to both those memorable auctions.

All these auctions were an unqualified success and would have been, I think, even if I'd sat on my backside and made little effort towards that success. The reason being that the general public, having only comparatively recently witnessed the purchase by the council of the main Tunnicliffe collection in its entirety, assumed, quite logically, that the auctions in Gaerwen were likely to be the very last chance it would get to purchase works by this popular artist for purely private enjoyment.

Works by Charles Tunnicliffe still do appear on the market, of course, with any works of an ornithological theme always proving popular. I often think, however, that the prices for Tunnicliffe's work at those auctions in 1985 and 1986 were much higher, on a relative scale, than the auction prices being achieved today, nearly thirty years on. Food for thought?

Clifford 'Cliff' William Jones OBE

With the obvious benefits of the new auction facility in Gaerwen and the success of the Tunnicliffe family collection, I was placing a much greater interest in the need to acquire consignments of quality, marketable paintings to sell on a regular basis. After all, the facilities were in place and second to none in the area at that time.

I cannot recall exactly how such a famous and much revered ex Welsh-international rugby star came to make contact with me; all I do recall is that it was to do with paintings and the sale and purchase thereof. The great Cliff Jones held a big interest in art and I have a feeling that he had purchased a painting or two at a particular auction of ours, after which the question of delivery was raised.

Cliff lived in Bonvilston, just outside Cardiff, at that time; I seem to recall that it was he who came up with a plan for us to meet somewhere half-way between north and south, and for me to take along with me Cliff's recent purchases; he would, in turn, bring some works up with him for me to take back to try and sell.

The plan worked well. We would meet in the car park of 'The Pound' at Leebotwood on the Wales/Shropshire border, have a snack and a quick refresher and put the world to rights before returning our separate ways. This plan was repeated on many occasions and enabled me to make the closer acquaintance of a lovely gentleman who had such a wide variety of interests.

Whenever he rang the office to arrange another delivery meeting, it was always "David, my boy, can we meet?" We continued using that same pub car park for many years and whenever I pass the spot on my way down to South Wales, I always think of the great Cliff Jones OBE.

'Not One of Mine,' by Kyffin Williams

Sometime in the 80s we had, at one of our monthly auctions, one or two sketches by Kyffin Williams, later of course to become Sir Kyffin Williams, but even back then, revered and loved by everyone who crossed his path. Many years later I was to get to know him quite well, certainly well enough to be able to appreciate his in-built generosity, particularly towards what he would have termed the 'ordinary person' as opposed to what he felt to be the pretensiousness of the 'establishment'.

On the viewing day in question, Kyffin's unmissable figure came in with a companion and made a bee-line for a small pencil sketch of a farmer, which had been fully catalogued as being by Kyffin Williams. He seemed to spend an inordinately long time over this work before declaring, in his magnificently stentorian 'Kyffin voice', for all to hear "Oh, no, definitely not one of mine".

Now what the great man had not realised, or possibly, had forgotten, was that this sketch had been given by him in exchange for dinner by the very person selling it at the auction! She was merely making a little space for a bigger and better work by him which she had recently acquired. Kyffin was apparently anxious to distance himself from a very quickly turned out 'doodle' which he obviously felt not to be fully up to the standard to which he was by then aspiring!

Following Sir Kyffin's sad death in 2006, I was instructed to carry out the necessary valuation work required by his executors. To be able to access the working environment of one of Wales' very best and much-loved artists was a privilege indeed.

Sheepdogs for Sale

In 1969, a meeting between four Anglesey farming friends took place at the, then very popular and iconic, eating hostelry known as The Castaways, situated in a remote corner of the island near Dwyran.

The Castaways' speciality menu was duck and very little else, but that did not matter as the owners, Mooney and

Morgan Evans about to commence the first auction of working sheepdogs. John Owen (left) and Iolo Owen (right).

Robin Damsell, cooked the best roast duck for miles, and you really had not lived without having bumped your way down the roughest lane imaginable to this cosy and very remote establishment. If a first-time visitor dared comment on the state of the Castaways' unsurfaced access highway, he/she would be given very short shrift by Robin and told to "take it or leave it".

His other 'speciality' in answer to a customer request for sight of the wine list was to look the customer straight in the eye with: " You're looking at it, red or white"?

Iolo Owen and a competitor studying sheepdog talent.

These owner's foibles were a well-known part of the character of The Castaways, for which many old customers will be saying today – "Thanks for the memories and all those morning-after hangovers"!

Back to the meeting of the friends. The Castaways as a venue was probably a cleverly thought-out ploy; a meeting of some twenty minutes' duration followed by a lot of chat and some imbibing lasting somewhat longer!

Iolo Owen, a very well-known and popular farmer and sheep breeder from Bodorgan with three friends John Owen, J D (Jackie) Williams and Richard (Dick) Ellis-Pritchard assembled to discuss the idea of conducting, by auction, a first-time-ever sale of working sheepdogs. This would be an unique auction and it was quickly agreed that if they could get Morgan Evans on board as auctioneer, the plan was certainly worth giving a try. Morgan duly agreed, with apparent little persuasion, so it was 'plan on'.

The auction was advertised for a Saturday in September 1969 and to take place on farmland at Fferam Bailey, Bodorgan, owned by Iolo. A very encouraging entry of some twenty sheepdogs turned up, watched by a very large crowd of slightly curious farmers unsure as to whether they were there to witness a one-off event or an important inaugural auction which would be soon copied by sheepdog enthusiasts and auctioneers throughout the Country.

The whole pleasing event was very low-key; there were no grandstands, barriers, microphones or any of the usual auction paraphernalia; just a nice, slightly sloping, open field with a wooden pen for the sheep at the far end.

I seem to recall that Morgan conducted the auction with a megaphone, but it was Iolo who had ensured that the prowess of the dogs would be suitably tested. He had agreed to provide a dozen or so sheep for the dogs to work, but it was soon realised that Iolo had picked out a troublesome bunch of four-legged woollies of the most awkward and hot-headed kind.

The auction progressed very well, but I do recall one or two young dogs, inexperienced but with good potential, ending up nearly in the adjoining farm having been completely flummoxed by those headstrong sheep. Their owners had long since lost control of their novices and the calm, controlled whistles and quiet commands had turned to shouts which could be heard in the next county!

Overall, this was a very successful inaugural auction and the majority of those present quickly realised that this was ground-breaking stuff which, undoubtedly, would be soon repeated in other parts of the country. They were right; in no time at all, the brilliant idea had been copied and very soon auctions of working sheepdogs were held in places as diverse as Bala and Sennybridge and eventually extending to several venues over the border.

But no matter, this had been a first auction ever of working sheepdogs and it had been held on the Isle of Anglesey. As far as prices are concerned, I seem to recall a top price on the day of some two hundred guineas (£210 in today's language), but at the low end, thirty to sixty guineas was probably nearer the average.

As I write this anecdote over forty-five years on, working sheepdog auctions are held everywhere and £10,000, yes, ten thousand pounds, was recorded for a working dog in 2013.

Just to think that the whole idea was thought out by those four farming friends sitting in The Castaways all those years ago!

To Pastures New

In 1982, I was appointed Acting Managing Director of Morgan Evans & Company which, by then, had become a limited company, a wise move bearing in mind the potentially huge financial liabilities which successful livestock auctioneers faced.

Later on in the 1980s the company had established itself as one of the three livestock auctioneers in the UK with the highest turnover of beef cattle. On a simple calculation of 800 cattle at £600 per head, this gives a one-day sales total of around half a million pounds without any regard for the three to five thousand lambs which would also be sold on the same day.

When it is considered that in those days the farmer picked up his proceeds cheque on the day of sale, whilst the auction company would wait for sometimes three weeks, before settlement by the buying company, the potential financial risk in such a fickle business is very easily appreciated.

For the next ten years, I very quickly came to realise what the role of acting managing director entailed. It became even more of a paper responsibility, as I was already heavily involved in auctioning both the fat and store cattle on two separate days each week as well as the organisation of both general and antique auctions. Add to this my work on the property side, carrying out valuations for building societies, solicitors and executors and the conducting of all agricultural and residential property auctions, and it will be appreciated that my every working day was always a full one

I really did thrive on this heavy volume of work and I have to say that Morgan, to his eternal credit, let me get on with things with little, or no, direct interference, except for those fairly rare occasions when a major policy decision had to be discussed.

The livestock market by now boasted roofs on both the cattle and sheep sections and the overnight facilities were second to none. From the very humble beginnings of the paddocks of a smallholding with sheep hurdles as pens to this modern, UK-renowned, livestock market facility in the space of about fifteen years, was no mean achievement.

If the tables had not already turned, then they were now turning at a rapid pace; Morgan Evans & Company had passed Bob Parry & Company on the outside lane and was unlikely to be ever caught up.

As the 1990s approached, I began to ask myself questions, fleeting ones at first but more serious as time went on. Approaching my half century, did I really see myself in this fairly high-pressure role perhaps ten years hence? Our three children Shân, John and Ben were completing their education at *Ysgol David Hughes* and were on their way to their further education and respective careers, so that family pressures were now lighter than they had hitherto been.

As the questions I was asking of myself, increased with seriousness and intensity, the answer to them came from an unlikely source – Brussels. Yet again, the long-suffering British farmer was to have imposed on him possibly the most far-reaching of all the often-crazy regulations imposed by London via Brussels.

Cattle were to have, in effect, identification passports and the movement of animals, even from one farm to another in the same ownership, was to be very strictly monitored and regulated. As we are all aware, new agricultural regulations, especially those imposed by Europe, invariably entail Brazilian forests of paperwork to add to the forests which the poor farmer and associated businesses already had to contend with.

The decision was made – I decided that I did not wish to be involved, even in sharing the burden of new regulations and paperwork on top of all the responsibilities which I already had, and these new rules were, undoubtedly just the thin end of the wedge and the forerunner of even more mind-boggling paperwork to come in the very near, and distant, future.

My notice, ending twenty-four years with Morgan Evans & Co., was handed in and duly accepted by Morgan with the understanding and dignity which were part and parcel of the character by which he was known to all and which had played a big part in his success over so many years.

I felt then, as now, that the debt owed by the North Wales agricultural community to Morgan Evans MBE should never, ever, be understated.

5

Colwyn Bay 1992

Knowing that the Colwyn Bay area was the ideal location in which to start up an auction business was one thing; finding that saleroom location was going to be a challenge, without any doubt. Having been brought up in the area, and with a mother who was an avid salegoer, I was confident that a saleroom was needed in order to uphold a long-held tradition in an area which still had in it plenty of 'old money' from over the industrialised English border.

Added to this theory was the fact that Phillips, the national auctioneers, had fairly recently vacated the town, leaving one or two auctioneers whose businesses were primarily on the estate agency side, but scarcely anyone else for whom regular auctions were a speciality.

There was one operator, however, who had held his last auction some two years prior to our arrival and with premises quite prominently situated on Abergele Road, close to the centre of town. He was John Pender, a dealer, a very experienced and well-known one at that, but who conducted auctions as well. In other words, he 'ran with the hare and hunted with the hounds,' as the saying goes. In the antiques world, this seldom, if ever, works out successfully.

I happened to notice in the local paper a small advertisement for Pender's auction premises and in no time at all we had taken the plunge and agreed to take the premises on a 3-year lease, with an option to purchase at the end of that period. Above the saleroom was a spacious 4-bedroomed flat with a less than salubrious view of the first floor apartments and rooftops of Colwyn Bay, but which was to be our place of residence for the next few years. A far cry from our very nice, modern bungalow in its own grounds in Star, Anglesey, but on the upside was to be the sheer convenience of living right above our new place of business.

So there we were, just two months or so on from a cushioned career on Anglesey, with the fairly urgent need to recommence the small matter of earning a living at the ripe old (or young ?) age of fifty, in our very own auction saleroom. Madness or confidence, I do not recall; probably a combination of both!

The premises had quite an interesting history; first as Thomas' Tea Rooms, where the ladies of the town and surrounds would meet for a reviving cuppa after some weekend shopping. In those days, Colwyn Bay's elegant shops held their own with any and were quite capable of satisfying the most discerning of customers. It then became one of the well-known chain of grocery shops called John Irwin, who were eventually swallowed up by none other than the ubiquitous Tesco. For once, a private company (ours) was following on from the retail giant as opposed to the other way around.

I am proud to state that over twenty years on, it is still Rogers Jones & Co. Auctioneers.

Our First Auction

After some frantic cleaning and decorating, helped by friends and relatives, and the purchase of a consignment of second-hand tables, we were ready for our first auction of antiques, to be held on 31st March 1992. The team in charge were Margaret (no previous auction experience), Margaret's sister and brother in law, Joy and Glyn Thomas from Mold (no previous auction experience) and a couple of porters.

Glyn's inexperience of auctions was more than made up

for by his having been a long-term and highly-respected National Provincial Bank manager. We were grateful for his financial experience and he and Margaret soon became an efficient team with an uncanny mastery of the pocket calculator.

We purchased a second-hand computer – sorry, its forerunner, a word processor, and printed and hand-stapled our own catalogues, and basically we were under starter's orders. We had somehow accumulated a very good and varied selection of 350 lots for our very first sale and were immensely encouraged by a full room and some very buoyant prices.

I particularly remember an entry of seven Royal Dux porcelain figurines which totalled nearly £4,000 including a pair of shepherd and shepherdess which alone realised a third of that sum.

We now had to keep the impetus going but need not have worried unduly; entries for our General Contents auctions soon began to tumble in and I am proud to state that from April 1992, we established, right at the outset, a pattern of three auctions every month – two general and one antique, and that pattern and regularity of sales continues to this day, over twenty years on, in 2014. Additional auctions do now also take place, such as quarterly Jewellery sales, twice-annual sales of Welsh art, (as well as two in Cardiff) and the occasional outside auction, as required.

Some two years after opening in Colwyn Bay, our landlord began gently harassing us to purchase the property, a year sooner than had been provisionally agreed. We duly reached agreement, and twelve months later we had engaged local builders to construct a rear extension to the saleroom as we were already finding space to be in very short supply indeed.

The *Lusitania* Sale

Towards the end of 1992, Andrew Morley, a respected local book dealer in Colwyn Bay, received a routine call to view some books for potential purchase at a gentleman's house in Lancashire. The books were very much to Andrew's liking and a deal was struck.

As he was leaving the house, the client, almost by way of a 'throw-away' question, asked Andrew if he 'knew of anyone who might be at all interested in that lot?' 'That lot' turned out to be a large chest full of paperwork relating to the Cunard and White Star Shipping Companies and, in particular, correspondence from various sources relating to the White Star liner *Lusitania*, which was torpedoed off the coast of Ireland in 1915 with the loss of nearly 1200 lives.

I still wonder how such a potentially important quantity of memorabilia came to be in the hands of one gentleman at his own home; my own conclusion was that he may have been an employee of Cunard's on the clerical side and that the paper shredder in his office was on the blink!

Andrew's experienced eye immediately saw the potential on offer and wasted no time in getting the chest and its contents down to us in Colwyn Bay. Sorting out and cataloguing all this fascinating, and sometimes chilling, paperwork was reward in itself and we arranged for it to be auctioned in January 1993. Approximately one half of the 535 lots in that auction were in the category 'Ocean Liner Memorabilia' and *Lusitania* items took up a considerable share of those.

Enquiries soon began to come in from far and wide, with many from the USA. Shortly before the auction Sky News rang to say that they had traced an elderly lady from the south of England who, as a young child, had survived the horrible sinking tragedy.

"Can a Sky crew please bring the lady up to Colwyn Bay

in order to film her poring over the *Lusitania* artefacts in the saleroom"?

"Of course," was the answer and the elderly lady duly came to be filmed, very sympathetically, in what was undoubtedly for her, a poignant and contemplative experience.

I quote, verbatim, just three lot descriptions from the *Lusitania* auction, in order to give some idea of what was involved:

> Lot 175: 'Handwritten Welsh letter on *Lusitania* headed paper by a gentleman from Coedpoeth, near Wrexham, to his brother on a journey out to America to make a new life. He describes life on board and the people on it.'
>
> Lot 190: 'Original telegram from the Pathological Institute in Milan to Cunard regarding method and cost of preserving human corpses from the *Lusitania*.'
>
> Lot 194: 'Correspondence from, and to, Cunard, regarding an original Rubens painting which a Mr Williamson was supposed to be bringing over on the *Lusitania*, entitled 'The Holy Family' and said to have cost £4,000.

Many of the lots found home buyers, particularly a prominent dealer from Southampton, but many items did end up 'over the pond', such was the world-wide interest in this auction.

I don't know if the *Lusitania* sale, coming as it did right at the beginning of 1993 and only twelve months after our inaugural auction, was to be a special omen.

Certainly, very soon afterwards, other 'specials' came our way. Firstly on 27th February in the following year we conducted a disposal auction at the Llandudno Motorcycle Museum of 'Vintage and Classic Motorcycles and Related Items.' The auction included a tantalising range of old bikes including Velocette, Sun Tourist, Excelsior, Sunbeam,

Royal Enfield and Triumph Trident, Tiger and Bonneville models, all ranging from 1919 to the 1960's. What an absolute enthusiast's delight. The smell of oil and overalls on that Saturday was wonderful, even to a non-motorcycle buff like me!

Then in May, we were favoured with instructions to conduct a studio sale of the works of the Conwy Valley artist Edwin James ('Ted') Dummet, 1906–1989. Some 180 original and varied works by this popular, well-travelled and well-exhibited artist were offered for sale at the Eagles Hotel in Llanrwst and without anything hitting the real heights, there was a satisfactory conclusion to the Saturday afternoon's proceedings.

Hotels For Sale
The last 15 years or so have seen the demise, or rather, the complete demolition, of three of the Colwyn Bay area's most iconic hostelries, all victims, one supposes, of the downturn in the fortunes of licensed premises. As an auction company, we were responsible for contributing, in a way, to the demise of these places of entertainment, having been instructed to dispose of their contents, by auction, on site.

The first, and for me personally, the most iconic of the three was the Ferry Hotel in Tal Y Cafn, occupying a truly idyllic position right on the river in a lovely part of the Conwy Valley. I remember it years ago as the place for locals to visit at a time when 'eating out' was not quite the taken-for-granted event it is today. I had my 21st birthday bash there in 1963, and I seem to recall that a good Saturday evening meal there in those days cost around 12/6d. Those, definitely, were the days!

Like all on-site auctions in business premises, the sadness of the auction at the Ferry in 1994 was no different.

Everything that was previously neat and tidy, in its functional place, was now gathered and bundled together for the convenience of customers visiting the place for entirely different reasons: to grab a memento and a bargain.

Pots and pans and well-worn tables and chairs do not usually set the world alight in auctions such as these, so it is quite easy to recall the highlight of the Ferry auction.

This was a large and rather impressive oil painting of the old Tal Y Cafn Ferry by Philip Osment, very much an unheralded, journeyman painter whose usual medium was watercolour. In this instance, however, he had really excelled himself with this massive and atmospheric depiction of the lovely rural scene which could be clearly seen from the front windows of the hotel. Two main bidders tousled it out over the painting which realised several hundred pounds, a figure far in excess of any I had previously obtained for works by Osment. I recall that this one lot alone accounted for a large portion of the total proceeds of the sale.

Despite the severe downturn in the fortunes of licensed premises by 2012, I feel certain that the Ferry Hotel would today, have bucked that trend and would have become, had it survived, one of the area's places to visit for a drink or a meal. There were few nicer locations in the whole of the Conwy Valley on a lovely summer's day!

'Ah, yes, I remember ...' are usually the first four words uttered by someone having his or her memory jogged by a visit or more to another of the area's most iconic hotels, the Hotel Seventy Degrees at Penmaenhead, on the old road out of Colwyn Bay and Old Colwyn towards Abergele.

Built in 1972, the Seventy Degrees, as it was so affectionately called, was a flat-roofed, flat-profiled, bungalow-looking hotel situated in a most fabulous position high up on the headland looking down on the complete magnificence of Colwyn Bay's sweeping coastline. On a really clear day one could probably see washing being hung out in the gardens of Douglas on the Isle of Man, with the Cumbrian Hills beyond.

I have no idea of the success of the Seventy Degrees over so many years, as a hotel where guests actually stayed and slept in a bed. I do, however, have just a little experience of this iconic hostelry as a 'function place', having attended, over a number of years both Round Table and Rotary dinners and Sportsman's Evenings there.

I recall one particular Sportsman's Evening when the guest speaker from Merseyside was rather well-oiled before he'd even got up to speak! One had apparently 'not lived' if one had not experienced, on the morning after a visit to Seventy Degrees, a dose of 'H, H and H,' or as a lucky victim might explain – a headache and one hell of a hangover!

The Seventy Degrees was to be demolished in 2007 to make way (how surprising) for yet more modern housing, although many years on, houses have not actually been built right on the site occupied by the hotel, but very close by. We received instructions in 2002 to deal with the disposal of the entire contents of the hotel and it all went very well despite the sadness of the occasion. There was an excellent attendance, not only of buyers, but also of locals with no intention of bidding for anything, but just wanting to pay a final visit, for old time's sake, to this most iconic of local hostelries.

The Rhos Abbey Hotel, right on the seafront in Rhos On Sea, all red brick, faux black-and-white panelling and stained glass windows, was built in 1898 and had become very much a landmark building up to the Millenium, in a seaside village which, with some justification, was beginning to acquire the 'chic' tag. Its landmark and iconic status, however, were not going to save yet another hotel from the demolition squad and it was replaced in 2001 by a block of apartments, whose construction did not quite come up to the appearance of the old hotel.

We conducted an auction of the contents on site in 2001 and, once again, nostalgia and pure business proved to be quite a mix, but on this particular occasion there was a demand for many of the constructional fixtures of the hotel, such as quality, 'real' wooden doors, stained glass windows and other fittings of a standard and workmanship worthy of the late 1900s.

Some ten years on, Rhos On Sea still has two seafront pubs and a third in the village. Will they all last the savage cuts now being perpetrated on our licensed premises?

Football Programmes

I received instructions one day from a lady in Kinmel Bay to go and see, with a view to selling, her late husband's collection of football programmes which he had amassed over a number of years. On being told that the collection was in 'the hundreds' I made very early arrangements to pop along to see them.

Not only had I a passing, personal interest in football, I was acutely aware of the wide demand for old British programmes, particularly those of pre-1950 vintage.

I always like to go to the middle pages to see the names on the team sheet, often to jog one's memory of a particular player and as a reminder of his exploits. Like Bert Trautmann OBE, the ex-German prisoner of war turned Manchester City goalkeeper, who broke his neck in the 1956 Cup Final and carried on playing to the final whistle. I had brief dealings with him when he lived in Benllech, Anglesey after his retirement.

Along I went to Kinmel Bay with great anticipation and enthusiasm, and was welcomed into the lady's bungalow with the words that 'they are all stored in the front bedroom.' And so they were, all in lovely condition in huge, neat piles on one of the divan beds.

I began to thumb through them carefully, keenly expecting to pick up an Everton programme or two, or one of the Manchester teams, or even a Wolves or a Cardiff City. Strangely, my first little handful, all shiny and immaculate, were Rotherham United, which I thought little of until I began to pick out more programmes at random from different parts of the piles in front of me; every one jack was a Rotherham United programme and as the lady owner began to notice my frustration, she asked, "Didn't I mention during my first call to you that all my husband's programmes were those of Rotherham United? We kept a pub near the ground for many years and the customers used to bring one in to my husband after every match!"

Now, I have nothing whatsoever against Rotherham United, nor indeed, Rotherham itself. Indeed, my son-in-law is a pure-bred Yorkshireman. But all I can state is that it was one very disappointed Welsh auctioneer who returned to his office in Colwyn Bay on that day!

On the subject of football, many years later I was to meet a truly interesting couple from the Bangor area who had many collecting interests, including jazz and other CDs, toy vehicles and football programmes and other related material. I could not help but admire the neatness and precision, not to mention the pride, which was apparent in their various collections, but it was their football story which left me open-mouthed.

Just prior to the formation of the present English Premier League in 1992, this non car-owning couple decided that they would attend a match at every one of the ninety-two football grounds in England and Wales, making up the four divisions of the Football League at that time.

They duly fulfilled their mammoth challenge in eighteen months and, in the process, managed to arrange a private audience with the legendary Brian Clough at Nottingham Forest. How many miles were covered in total, and how many thousands of pounds were added to the coffers of the Country's bus and train companies during this footballing adventure, would be pure guesswork.

Taking pride of place in their hallway is a case containing a badge for every one of the 92 football clubs whose matches this couple took so much trouble to visit!

Grand Piano For Sale – Handle With Care!
Most of us, I'm sure, will agree that there are few more elegant musical instruments than top-of-the-range, European made, grand pianos in quality rosewood or walnut cases.

Admiring a grand piano is one thing; having the space to accommodate one in a 'normal' sized property proves to be the sticking point for many a household. Despite the various sizes of 'grand' – Baby, Boudoir and Full Concert Grand – this type of piano can take up an awful lot of room.

Condition of both the movement and case is all-important. One of the commonest faults one sees is fading and bleaching to the case caused by long exposure to natural light. The sad part is that such fading will always be severe and in a concentrated, relatively confined area on the case. The reason is quite simple and obvious – once a grand piano of any size is given its place in a room of the house, it will invariably be given a spot by a window, after which the houseowner will be very disinclined to move it around just to give it a bit of a dusting.

Sadly, since well after the turn of the Millenium, the market for any traditional pianos, be they upright or grand, has taken quite a severe downturn. Changes in life-style, the advent of portable, space-saving keyboards, coupled with Mr Yamaha making pianos in the Far East, have all conspired to reduce the popularity of the traditional type of instrument. Thankfully, the demand has still held from professionals and purists for the 'Premier League' instruments made by the likes of Steinway, Bechstein and Bluthner.

I regret the demise in demand for the traditional upright piano. Whenever there was one on offer in the saleroom we'd be guaranteed on one of the viewing days to have someone give a nice quick tinkle of the keys, and it was often quite evident from the standard of tinkling that they'd done it before.

Several years ago, in 1998 I think, the office received instructions to dispose of a nice quality grand piano located at a country house in the Conwy Valley. 'Grands' were still in vogue and this was a particularly nice, well-maintained rosewood example by a respected Paris maker. No fading and in fine tune, this grand would sell well, I felt. The piano was duly removed to the saleroom and given the usual pre-sale advertising plug which such a good instrument warranted.

I pause at this juncture, as the word 'removed' has a rather important connotation in the world of grand pianos. It may not be fully realised that, unlike an ordinary upright piano which can be normally removed bodily on a trolley by four muscular men, a grand really does require removal by specialists who know the 'piano ropes'.

Basically, the whole body of the grand piano has to be carefully supported whilst the legs and the pedal assembly are detached from it. It is then carefully tipped into the vertical position, then to be blanketed and placed in a form of cradle on wheels which ensures its safe removal and transportation. The slightest tumble or nudge could so easily cause very expensive damage to such a delicate, but at the same time, heavy instrument.

Our Conwy Valley grand was given due prominence in the antique auction catalogue and realised a very satisfactory hammer price of around £3,000.The purchaser was a lady with farming connections somewhere in the Denbighshire hinterland a few miles from Colwyn Bay. She revealed that her lovely, newly-acquired Paris grand piano was ultimately destined, coincidentally, for a daughter living on the outskirts of Paris itself. In the meantime, it would be removed from the saleroom to the farm.

On the day after the auction, referred to by us, as 'collect-and-clear-up day', we were busying ourselves with post-sale tasks when a good looking 'hunk' of a young man breezed into the saleroom. By 'hunk' I mean tall and nearly as wide and agriculturally muscular.

With little, or no, preamble, he came straight out with the declaration that "we've come for the piano." In unison, three of us replied, "How do you mean, you've come for the piano, to which piano are you referring?" (assuming that he must surely have come to the wrong place).

"The big piano which my mother bought from you yesterday" was the hunk's reply. He was serious.

Thinking that some light relief would be appropriate, one of us asked, "Moving it on your own, are you?"

He replied, much more seriously "No, there are four of us." He gestured towards the pavement outside, where we caught sight of three more hunks from the same mould waiting for instructions from their chief.

Realising that the visit by these four front-row forwards had a serious purpose to it, one of us enquired as to the mode of transport chosen for this lovely musical instrument.

"Over there, no problem," was the immediate reply, as hunk number one pointed to a parked vehicle just a few yards down from the saleroom.

A cattle truck of the very large variety, commonly seen loading and unloading cattle and sheep at most livestock markets around the county, had already got its tailboard down in readiness to receive this £3,000 piece of musical instrument precision.

In fairness, they had gone to the bother of giving the floor of the truck a good thick layer of quite fresh straw of which any self-respecting Welsh Black bullock would have been well satisfied.

We all stared, open-mouthed, as the gang of hunks marched into the saleroom and proceeded to give the piano an assessment lasting about three seconds before the order came from the chief hunk: "*iawn hogia, pawb yn barod amdani?*" (alright lads, everyone ready for it?)

There was to be no dismantling, no detaching of the lid, or of the legs and pedal assembly. Sheer muscle power was the order of the day as each of the removers chose a side of the piano which they lifted together as the word was given. We all stood with bated breath as some shuffling and tipping took place as the valuable cargo passed through the saleroom doorway, which was slightly narrower than the piano itself.

The lovely French grand piano was carried up the tailboard of the truck and placed reasonably ceremoniously on its bed of Welsh straw without even being tied down. The tailboard was closed as it had been hundreds of times before and the four hunks were off with a quick thanks and a wave.

In fifty two years, I do not recall ever, ever seeing any piano, grand or other, transported in this way. Chopin would have turned in his grave!

Distance No Object

One of our oft-quoted selling points at our Colwyn Bay saleroom is that we are always prepared to travel anywhere, and any distance, to see and assess clients' goods for potential sale or evaluation for anyone for a variety of purposes – insurance, probate, gift tax and potential sale etc. During one fairly routine office day during late Autumn 2009, I took a phone call from a gentleman in Anglesey. The conversation went something like this:-

"I understand that you carry out valuations for potential sale purposes and wondered whether I could forward you a photograph of a rather nice Welsh tridarn." (The word means '3 pieces', comprising a base cupboard, a middle section, usually with very attractive smaller cupboards, both sections then being topped with a galleried hood. Tridarns are usually in heavy oak and date from the early to mid-18th century period.)

"No problem," I replied, "but rather than having to assess the merits of such a potentially valuable piece from a photograph, it would be far better if I could come up to see the tridarn in the flesh."

"I am afraid that would not be possible as I do not have the piece here," was the reply.

I responded immediately with the declaration that 'distance was no object at all.' After all, I pointed out, Anglesey was but a 'short hop down the road'. He was having none of it, and sensing a creeping exasperation on my part he then revealed that the tridarn was his brother's in whose home it was located – in New Zealand of all places!

My mischievous mind raced quickly as I considered how to respond to his revelation. "Just one moment whilst I reach for my diary". I left a suitable pause in the conversation before continuing. "What part of New Zealand does your brother reside in?"

"Blenheim, in South Island," came the reply.

"Ah yes, I know it well," said I, wondering just where he felt the conversation was going.

"How would the week beginning January 4th suit your brother?" I asked the temporary wall of silence at the end of the line.

"You mean you are actually going to be passing Blenheim on that date and that you could call to see the tridarn then?"

"Absolutely," said I, triumphantly, having already planned a holiday to New Zealand and so the arrangement was duly finalised with my agreeing to make contact with his brother upon our arrival at South Island.

I duly saw the tridarn in New Zealand as arranged, but unfortunately the outcome was not quite the icing on the cake that I would have wished. It transpired that the owner had purchased the piece some ten years previously at an auction in Auckland, to where it had been shipped from Australia. With market prices for old oak having taken quite a tumble in the last few years, my valuation of the tridarn only just about equated to what the owner had paid for it in Auckland all those years ago.

Never mind, at least we were able to prove that our 'distance no object' claim was a genuine one!

Toast to a Hero

As a sequel to the New Zealand anecdote, I should also mention a thrilling encounter which occurred right at the commencement of our stay there.

We had flown into Auckland and had decided on a few days' rest and recuperation in the City before setting off on what was to be a fairly arduous itinerary.

On the morning after our arrival at a city centre hotel, Margaret and I had gone down for breakfast to the lower-level ground floor of the hotel when I noticed a lot of activity in the foyer area with lots of carrying-in of cameras and sound equipment and many small groups of men all in black blazers chatting earnestly.

I looked at one weather-beaten but fit-looking gentleman and realised that his blazer also had on it the famous tell-tale white fern which is the renowned logo of the New Zealand All Blacks rugby team.

It transpired that the hotel was the venue for the press release and announcement that morning of the various towns in New Zealand which were to host all the preliminary rounds of the 2011 Rugby World Cup.

Having taken in all that, I thought little more of it until we entered the designated breakfast room. It was full of All-Blacks past and present, including the coaches Graham Henry and Steve Hansen.

Taking all this in and having enjoyed the hearty cooked breakfast, I proceeded to the centre table containing all the various breads on offer and the large toasting machine: the rather ponderous, Heath Robinson affair where you place your chosen chunk of bread, hopefully without scorching fingers, onto the revolving grill and then just hang around hoping that all those in the queue know which piece, or pieces, of bread are theirs.

I suddenly became aware of what I can only describe as the shadow of the figure of a large gentleman just behind me who appeared to be studying rather intently the machinations of the toasting apparatus.

"I'm sorry to bother you, but would you have any idea how this contraption works?" I turned to him, immediately realising that talking to me was none other than the great Colin ('Pine Trees') Meads, one of New Zealand's legendary former All Blacks.

Not realising that I must have looked like a toasting machine expert, I quickly gathered my wits about me and mumbled something about being a humble Welshman in such exalted company and proceeded, as slowly as I could, as I wanted to savour the moment, to explain to the great Colin Meads how this piece of toasting machine worked.

As he thanked me, he took my hand, enveloped it as if he were squeezing a lemon and wished us both well on our holiday. I seem to recall that several days later my right hand still tingled from this great man's handshake.

I did wonder at the time, if there were any means of preserving, for posterity, the handshake of such a famous sporting icon. I should not like to have been tackled by him!

Fill up your chests!

I don't know just how many chests of drawers must have passed through my hands over a fifty-year career. There will have been a very varied and vast selection from Jacobean to Georgian, to William, Victorian and Edwardian and even to as recent as the 1930s. All in a variety of wonderful, lovingly-worked timbers such as walnut (the purists' favourite), rosewood, mahogany, oak and even the ubiquitous pine, beloved today of so many younger furniture buyers.

The auction of one chest of drawers in particular sticks in my memory, not so much for high value which it had not, nor because of any history of note to do with it. No, simply because of the quite hilarious post-sale consequences arising from its disposal.

I had sold for quite a decent price at one of our auctions in Colwyn Bay a particularly nice quality, beautifully-proportioned small mahogany chest of drawers from the 1840s (William iv) period. It was in lovely order, attractively coloured, and had come in for sale from an impeccable source. The hammer price was about £1100 and was sold to a retired army brigadier who was a good, if not frequent, buyer at the saleroom. He was the sort of absolutely straight, no-nonsense type of customer who treated you in exactly the way he would expect to be treated at all times by the staff and myself.

The brigadier lived some eighteen miles from the saleroom, so at his request we arranged for the chest to be delivered to his home for an agreed modest charge, by one of our local carriers. All went well and the chest, as far as I was aware, was duly delivered to the brigadier's home without a hitch.

Several days went by, before I received a request in the saleroom to take an incoming phone call from the brigadier concerning his recently-purchased chest of drawers. My mind raced into top gear as cold shudders ran down my spine. My immediate, panicky reaction was to buy time, lots of it, whilst I tried to work out just what it might be troubling the brigadier. I shouted to my colleague –

"Tell him I'm out of the office for five minutes and I'll ring him back."

I badly needed those five minutes to get my mind sorted and to try and imagine, in a worst-case-scenario, what horrific accident had befallen the brigadier's chest of drawers. Had the removers damaged the chest or damaged the paintwork as it was being moved into the house, or had a leg, or more seriously still, another part of the chest fallen off or been damaged in some other catastrophic way? What on earth could have happened to this lovely piece of furniture to cause its new owner to want to make a special phone call to me about it?

My mind continued racing and by the time I picked up the phone to return the brigadier's call, I had formulated in my mind answers, excuses, reasons – call them what you will – to the questions about to be fired at me by the brigadier. Another problem I had was that the brigadier himself, whilst of absolutely impeccable character, was not endowed with an apparent sense of humour, being as he was, of a very reserved and quiet nature.

The time had now come to pick up the phone and return his call, praying, as I did so for some miracle, and, at the same time, hoping that some polite small talk would suitably set the tone for whatever dressing down I was about to receive.

"Ah, Rogers-Jones (I hadn't got a rank, so this was how I was addressed), good of you to call me back, keeping all right and busy are we?" and before I had a chance to answer, he continued – "Thought I'd give you a ring about the old chest I bought from you the other day." Oh hell, I thought, here comes the dressing down or whatever it was I was about to have to endure.

"Got it delivered safely and all that, super set of chaps you organized for me, no problem at all, they placed the chest on the landing as requested and it takes its place magnificently, absolutely pleased as punch with the whole thing." I was saying nothing but thinking a lot – when on earth was he going to deliver the crushing blow instead of all this small talk?

"There's only one thing," here comes the killer blow at last, "The lady and I began last weekend to give the chest a bit of a dusting and some fresh lining paper to the drawers, when we discovered within the top drawer a further, small secret drawer. I really am sorry to bother you Rogers-Jones, I know you're a terribly busy chap, but do you think the previous owner will be anxious for the return of the rather fine set of dentures we found in the secret drawer?"

I was certain that I detected a slight guffaw from the brigadier, who had put me through such agonies, as he concluded with, "All the best old boy, let me know if he does, will you?"

A set of dentures is one thing, but a chest fairly full of

many personal and artistic artefacts belonging to the estate of the late Sir Kyffin Williams is, I would suggest, a rather different matter.

This slightly unfortunate episode occurred concerning a chest of drawers which was sold, amongst other items, by the beneficiaries of the great artist's estate shortly after his death in 2006. The fairly standard Victorian piece formed part of the entire, traditional contents of his lovely cottage on the Menai Strait.

The contents were directed by the beneficiaries to be sold at an auction house outside Wales. Unfortunately, it would appear that neither the beneficiaries nor the auctioneers appeared to have taken the trouble to check the interior of the chest, prior to sale, whereupon an eagle-eyed dealer bought the piece on the assumption that the numerous contents, some of a personal, and others of an artistic nature, were going to be his 'bargain of the century' on being resold by him elsewhere at a later date.

It had to be pointed out to the not-so-lucky buyer that all the pieces in the chest formed part of an important legacy to another beneficiary, but it took the threat of an injunction to prevent the sale of the items before the sad episode was, eventually, resolved.

No Smoking!

Exhortations and advice concerning our smoking habits are usually the remit of our namby-pamby powers that be. Not that I don't agree that smoking does damage our health and leads to very many premature deaths.

But what, you may ask, is an auctioneer doing adding his penn'orth to the no-smoking campaign? Well, it's like this. Not only does the by-product of smoking, nicotine, cause damage to our lungs, this sticky, oily by-product of 'dragging on a fag' can cause untold damage to works of art, in particular to oil paintings on canvas, which are not normally protected by sheets of glass.

I have, on many occasions been asked to comment on, and value, clients' cherished art possessions only to have to produce a long pessimistic face, as soon as the work is presented for inspection and analysis. It does not really take an expert to determine when a painting has been subjected to prolonged exposure to nicotine. The overall yellow, even sometimes sticky feel to the work tells one immediately what the painting has suffered. "Was uncle/aunt/mother a smoker?" I would ask gently and the somewhat embarrassed answer would invariably be in the affirmative.

All is not lost, however. Art restoration experts can, and do, perform miracles on badly-neglected works of art but, and it's a big but, such complex and painstaking restorative operations come at very considerable cost to the owner. Such cost will very often exceed the actual value of the painting itself, which can be sad and distressing in the case of a much-cherished family heirloom and leaves an owner with the dilemma – to restore or not to restore?

I vividly remember going to visit the workshops of an art restorer who was nearing the completion of a restoration project on a rather good oil painting, badly nicotine-affected, but very attractive and potentially quite valuable. "Look at this", the restorer beckoned, showing me a large jar of what, at first glance, looked like motor engine oil. "Smell that", which I did – thick liquid nicotine which he had expertly coaxed off the canvas – and I remember wondering just how many of the smoking population would vow there and then to stop their habit at the sight of the contents of that awful jar!

Smoking and nicotine are never selective in the way they affect our possessions. Soft furnishings often come into the saleroom from a smoking household and the effect on their value can be enormous, with a tell-tale lingering smell giving the game away to potential buyers.

I remember visiting the property of a widowed lady on Anglesey who had retired to a residential home. Her house was well-furnished throughout with good-quality, potentially very saleable, modern items and it was evident that she needed the best possible prices as a contribution to her care costs.

As soon as I entered the house, took in the smoky smell and saw the heavily yellowed walls and ceilings, it became immediately obvious that her situation was potentially dire. There was not the slightest prospect of a customer for such heavily contaminated furnishings and the attendant removal costs would have placed an even heavier financial burden on the lady.

The sad sequel to this story is that the entire contents of this property were eventually disposed of, other potential buyers having been called in but having declined to make a single penny offer for them.

Smoking kills. It also has a rather bad effect on our possessions!

Breaking Up is Hard to Do

I have long lost count of the number of frustrating occasions, when visiting householders, I have found myself listening to awkward reasons as to why a certain piece of furniture, a pair of valuable jugs, a pair of silver candlesticks or a set of six valuable chairs, are no longer standing in front of me as their careful makers intended – complete – as a pair or as a set, thus properly fulfilling their maximum potential.

I remember a call I made to a house in Llandudno where, amongst an array of fairly ordinary contents, was a very fine quality Georgian silver candlestick by a prominent silversmith of the period. The client clearly wanted to sell the candlestick, but I almost sensed his hope that I was not going to ask him the obvious and rather, inevitable question.

"Did you ever recall seeing the missing partner to the one standing in front of us?" Yes, he did, and not only that, he knew where the missing candlestick was now – at the house of a distant cousin in Devon. A shake of the head was the answer to my query as to the chances of the cousin agreeing to a reunion of these two fine pieces of silver.

I therefore proceeded to complete the routine paperwork for the entry of the candlestick into one of our auctions. I was asked to recommend a reserve price and came up with a figure in the region of £500.

I suddenly thought, before leaving, that I would attempt one last throw of the dice. If he would be willing to seek his cousin's permission to allow me to make contact with her, I would give her the 'full sales patter' to try and persuade her to part with her candlestick, and to participate with her cousin in what I would promise to be an highly profitable financial result.

Permission, to my slight surprise, was duly given to make contact with the cousin in Devon, but on speaking to her, I found myself slightly on the wrong foot from the very start. "I understand that you've only valued my cousin's candlestick at £500. £1,000 between us will hardly buy us a Caribbean cruise!" I was rather firmly told.

That's it, I'm in there, I said to myself, barely able to hide my delight at the coup de grace I was about to deliver. 'If I were more or less to guarantee the two of you a minimum of £3,000 for the pair at our auction, how would that satisfy?"

I could almost hear the sound of her smile on the telephone and very quickly I was given permission to offer the sticks as a pair, which was exactly what such fine workmanship deserved.

Thereafter, everything really was on my side; such good

quality pairs of candlesticks just do not come up for auction every day of the week. The day of the auction duly arrived and I knew that one of the most saleable lots on offer that day would be the pair of Llandudno-via-Devon candlesticks which realised a nice, hefty £4,400.

The very obvious moral to this story is that under no circumstances can the splitting up of sets or pairs of valuable antiques be justified. But this is exactly what families do get up to. And when doing so, they are usually unaware of the very simple, unwritten rule, which is that one half of a pair or set is not going to be worth 50 per cent of the potential value of the complete item!

I have been witness to this type of 'offence' on so many occasions. The most bizarre example I recall, was at a house in Llanberis where my gaze was drawn towards the very obvious base of a Victorian mahogany bookcase cupboard, or, '*Cwpwrdd Gwydr*' taking pride of place in the parlour despite the give-away bare timber on the top of the cupboard, which would normally have been concealed by the top section whose presence was definitely not obvious.

"Where is the top," I asked outright, and without any hesitation or obvious embarrassment, I was calmly told that it was at her sister's in Bangor, the cupboard having been left to the two by their late mother!

Chairs, the poor things, are so often the victims of our ill-considered deliberations when it comes to that dreaded procedure amongst families known as 'sharing out' or 'dividing up'. When will the public learn that dining chairs are saleable only if in fours, sixes, or any other even denomination? "Sorry", I often have to say to families with disappointed looks on their faces, 'ones, twos and threes in chairs are seldom of value unless they happen to match similar, if not identical, chairs in their possession.'

It is occasions like this that sometimes make me a very

frustrated auctioneer. Breaking up should be hard to do!

Just a Russian Plate

In 2008, an elegant elderly lady client from the Bangor area asked me to visit her as, 'she was just a little concerned that her cleaner was struggling to reach ornaments on some of the higher shelves which might cause damage, not only to the ornaments, but to the cleaner herself.'

I duly called to see her and after some delightful chat and reminiscing, she invited me to take a look along the whole of the high wall shelf running around the walls of her very elegantly furnished lounge, to confirm whether there was anything that particularly stood out.

I ventured the opinion that all the ornaments displayed

Just a Russian plate

were of a very nice, saleable quality, but that if she was to be concerned regarding potential damage to any particular item, that might be to a very nice-looking circular plate which took my eye. On pointing this plate out to her, she ventured that it had been purchased by her much-travelled late husband whilst in Russia and that he always had a keen eye for anything of good quality.

A step ladder was obtained for one slightly nervous auctioneer to gently lift the plate from its hitherto safe and lofty perch high up on the wall. Upon inspection and after some impromptu research, this porcelain plate of absolutely sumptuous quality and in magnificent condition with not a single scratch, was felt to be by The Imperial Porcelain Manufactory of Russia and was originally from the Raphael Service and carried the date of 1898.

Faithfully promising the client that her plate was going to realise a 'substantial sum of money' it was agreed for me to take it back to the saleroom for further research. To our delight, an identical plate, nine and a half inches exactly, in diameter, had been fairly recently sold at one of the big London auction houses for a hefty £12,000.

The good news was duly conveyed to one delighted lady, with the comment that if her plate made anywhere near that sort of money she would be 'over the moon'.

The superb Russian plate from Bangor received the fullest and most prominent treatment from us in Colwyn Bay and appeared in the auction of 27th May 2008 as Lot 183. Interest in this gem of an item came from far and wide and to everyone's great delight it achieved a resounding hammer price of £19,000.

Not only was our lovely, elderly client 'over the moon', so were we!

Medals for Heroes

I know that many fellow auctioneers in the UK sell war medals by auction on a pretty regular basis, fuelled by the excellent demand from the numerous serious collectors that exists for these items.

During my years in Colwyn Bay, I have experienced the privilege of offering by auction four Military Crosses by various local holders of this very distinguished award. A Victoria Cross would, of course be the ultimate goal of an auctioneer, but four Military Crosses are more than adequate to give one an appreciation of the exploits and sheer, seemingly fearless, bravery of all those British service personnel who deserve our thanks and admiration.

In September 2011, I received instructions from a lady in Anglesey to sell by auction medals which had been awarded in the First World War to a distant relative from Birkenhead on the Wirral.

It would be an injustice and, I feel, an insult, if I were to condense, to the slightest degree, the catalogue description for the sale of not only the military medal, but also the military cross, of Sergeant Robert George Wills of Birkenhead. Anyone not moved to tears on reading the following exploits must have a very hard streak in them.

Lot 3 in the auction:

Sergeant Robert Wills, 9 Taunton Park Road, Birkenhead – enlisted August 14th 1914 as a signaller with the Cheshire Regiment –

His cased MILITARY MEDAL and RIBBON and his London Gazette/War Office citation reads: 'no.452152 Acting Sergeant Wills of the 11th Signal Company, Royal Engineers – South of Oostaverne, for gallantry when in charge of brigade Advanced Post, near Mahieu Farm from 7th June 1917. He directed the line of wires under fire and opened and maintained signal stations on several occasions when wires were smashed by shellfire.'

His cased MILITARY CROSS and War Office citation reads – 'to Second Lt Robert George Wills M.M. Royal Engineers attached to the 46th Division Signal Company Royal Engineers – on the night 3rd/4th. October 1918 at Magny-la-Fosse he showed great gallantry and devotion to duty when a 5.9 gas shell having burst in his signal office, killing and wounding all the staff in the office at the time and interrupting communication. With one sapper he restored communication and worked both as operator and lineman through a most difficult period until relieved next day'.

A letter from the Deputy Military Secretary at the War Office, dated 28th July 1919 to Lt Wills' parents in Birkenhead enclosing both his Military Medal and Military Cross. Lt Wills was repatriated but subsequently died of his injuries.

His three General Service Medals are included together with his Volunteers Medal and ribbon, also his death plaque and 1914 Christmas tobacco tin, two photographs of him in uniform and a photograph of him (extreme right in the photograph) and his fellow men washing in the outdoors at Abergavenny Camp in south Wales).

The hammer price which this lot achieved is freely available on line. I am deliberately omitting reference to it from this anecdote as I would not wish it to be seen to being given more prominence than the fantastic and sobering achievements of this young soldier.

In the early 90s, I was instructed by a local solicitor to visit an elderly gentleman in Old Colwyn to discuss the disposal of one or two pieces. "When you go there," he urged, "ask him, if he's in a good mood, to tell you about his George Medal" (the civilian version of the Victoria Cross).

He lived alone and I immediately sensed that here was a

candidate for a good heart-to-heart chat. As soon as we had warmed to one another, I broached the subject of his George Medal. Now you would think that he was relating the story of a recent visit to the supermarket on a rainy day, such was the modest and almost nonchalant, manner with which he began to relate what was turning out to be a barely credible tale of reckless bravery.

He was on duty one day as a Platoon Leader in one of Birmingham's Home Guard detachments when he was alerted to a burning incendiary device having fallen and landed on a giant gasometer right in the centre of a densely populated residential area.

Without a second's hesitation, he climbed up the vertical steel ladder to the top of the gasometer and somehow extinguished and/or removed the burning device, thus preventing the possible total destruction of a very large chunk of Birmingham. I seem to recall that this wonderful old soldier ended his story with: "That's all there was to it really." Incredible but true!

Accents and Dialects

I consider myself to be a bit of a student in what might be called the observational art of accents and dialects. I love accents themselves, some more than others. I suppose we all have our favourites; amongst mine are Geordie and Scouse, the latter sometimes not easy to understand but the (invariably witty) owners have a character of their own and are the salt of the earth. Oh,and I nearly forgot, our own 'Made in Wales' is not a bad one either!

I am by no means an expert on the subject, but I am able to 'place' at least six accents for areas located in the relatively short distance between Aberdaron and Wrexham. I am sure there are more in smaller, inland pockets which locals in those areas, and experts on the subject, will be more familiar with than I.

In 1996, a recently widowed Lancastrian lady, who had relocated to the Abergele area, called to enquire if we were interested in handling the disposal of her late husband's library of specialist books.

I duly paid her a visit to see what turned out to be a collection of about 300 books, all lovingly amassed over quite a number of years and, so surprisingly, almost all having the identical subject matter – accents, dialects and surnames mainly relating to the county of Lancashire.

Knowing less about the subject matter than I have since learned, I was rather lost for words when the time came to proffer advice and my professional opinion as to the likely prospects for the collection under the hammer, bearing in mind what I perceived to be a rather narrow subject field.

The client took on board my views and declared that she wanted the book collection sold regardless of its prospects as she had not the room to keep them nor any particular interest in what had, after all, been her late husband's exclusive pastime.

I need not have worried at all regarding the collection's potential on the open market. Collectors and keen students of the subject homed in from all parts of the UK and even from the States to ensure the success of the sale.

The collection was catalogued into fifty lots with a top price of £925 for Lot 317 – 'A large number of sundry books on Saddleworth, Shaw, Marsden and the Oldham area'.

'Sketches and Rhymes in the Rochdale Dialect' by J T Clegg and 'Glossary of Rochdale with Rossendale Words and Phrases' by Henry Cunliffe realised £280 and 'Folk Speech of East Yorkshire' with one or two other books, made £110.

The collection totalled a very satisfactory £6,000 proving, if proof were needed, that sometimes the most seemingly diverse of subjects can elicit quite unexpected demand and interest. Such has been the continued interest in this particular specialist subject, I am confident that, by 2014, eighteen years on, this nice library would have well exceed this figure.

But our client was more than happy with the outcome of her late husband's collection all those years ago.

Murder Most Foul (2)

On 25th November 2001, an elderly widow living alone was hideously and brutally murdered in her bungalow home in the Upper Village of Llanfairpwll on Anglesey. Her attacker was a local youth, apparently fascinated with, and obsessed by, vampires and the like. He was found guilty of what was, mildly (in my opinion) described as a 'callous and brutal attack.'

A short while after the terrible event, I received a telephone call from a solicitor in Llangefni acting in the lady's estate. His exact words were "You've been mentioned in the late Mrs ... will" and as he 'heard' my 'puzzled silence' at the other end of the line, he quickly added, "before you become too excited, I should add that you were appointed by her to carry out the valuation of her goods and chattels for probate purposes in the event of her death."

He went on to say that I was to make contact with one of the detectives handling the case in order to gain access to the bungalow. This I duly did and arranged to meet the officer at the property at an agreed time. On arrival, I was handed a pair of gloves and ordered, not asked, not to touch anything during the course of my inspection of the contents of the property.

I fully understood the reason for this request, but after forty years carrying out similar valuations, I felt it to be a bizarre and somewhat surreal situation. Never before had I been asked to value items in a property on a 'glance only' basis without being able to feel or touch, and I very quickly found myself hoping that such a situation would never arise again, in view of the horrific circumstances surrounding the death of one innocent, elderly lady.

Olympic Heroine (2)

Sometime in 2008, I received instructions to call on a lady and gentleman at their property in Rhos On Sea.

On being invited in, my usually inquisitive eye led me, in the hallway of the house, to an array of excellent photographs on the walls, which did not require an expert to realise that they all related to athletics. Also amongst them was a framed title 'London Olympics 1948.'

The very first photograph on the wall depicted a female athlete breaking the tape at a track event. Having a bit of a general interest in most forms of sport, I enquired if the winning lady was the famous Dutch runner, Fanny Blankers-Koen. "Yes, quite right," was the reply, "and the one shown coming in second behind her in the photograph was me."

You could, as they say, have knocked me down with a feather on hearing this snippet, delivered, as it was, in such throwaway fashion. The lady of the house, Mrs Audrey Mitchell, was, in her athletic days, Audrey Doreen Swayne Williamson, who won that silver medal at the London Olympics all those years ago in 1948.

To be placed second in an Olympic Games event to the famed Fanny Blankers-Koen was some achievement, especially when it is realised that in those 1948 Games alone, the Dutch athlete won no fewer than four gold medals. (Oh, by the way, she was four months pregnant at the time, with her third child)!

But once again, as with my previous 'Olympic Heroine' anecdote, it was the totally modest way used by Mrs

Mitchell in recollecting her achievement that took my breath away and left me totally lost in my admiration of her.

I think that I eventually got down to talking the business which I had originally been asked to do, but it was very difficult to drop the subject of those Olympic Games as Mrs Mitchell revealed snippets of her exploits in such a disarming way.

Sadly, Mrs Audrey Mitchell passed away in April 2010.

Good Collections – and Bad Ones

Collecting 'things' has always been part and parcel of the antique and auction scene. The extent, and range, of items collected by people is truly amazing and far too extensive to begin listing in detail.

I touch briefly on a list of collectables which clients of Rogers Jones & Co. indulge in – pigs, chickens and elephants are firm favourites in the animal category. Egg cups, thimbles, moustache cups and toast racks are a favourite in the china category. All these are items which can be collected without breaking the bank. On a slightly higher value level, silver vestas (match holders), silver vinaigrettes and other small, Georgian silver items across the board are popular items which spring to mind. But the list is exhaustive and I never cease to be amazed when I hear of 'yet another subject' which a client has seen the future in as a collectable subject.

Collecting is a continuously turning wheel; as something new is suddenly brought to the notice of the public, so it has the potential there and then to commence being a collectable item. The secret, of course is to anticipate, ahead of the competition, when something new presents itself as a future small pot of gold.

I have two distinctly personal views on 'collecting'; the good and the bad. There is the good collecting as outlined above, of items from shops, fairs and auctions carried out by a collector who has made his or her own mind up as to what to collect and how much financial outlay is to be involved.

There is then, what I call, the bad collecting which often is indulged in by the elderly. This is what I term the 'hard sell' collecting, often encouraged by companies of doubtful repute who carry full page glossy coloured advertisements in newspapers and whose 'blurb' contains boasts regarding the 'investability' of their product – which is seldom likely to be fulfilled.

'Limited Editions' are two words which, sadly, see far too many people reaching for their cheque books before fully reading the, sometimes extensive, small print in these cleverly composed advertisements. Some of those collectors' wall plates are very much a case in point; I am well aware that most collectable ceramics have dropped in value during the last eight years or so. But some of these so-called 'collectors' plates have never had the potential to appreciate in value, simply because they are so badly made. I deliberately use the word 'some' because there are collectors' plates, notably those by Wedgwood, Royal Copenhagen and Coalport, to name a few, whose products are of good quality and have held their values reasonably well despite downward trends.

I leave what I consider to be the saddest aspect of 'collecting' to the very last. There must be a medical term to describe what I, in lay-person terms, describe as 'addictive compulsive buying', but I don't know what that medical term might be. All that I do know is that when one comes across it, as I have done on quite a few occasions, the result can be a distressing and mind-boggling sight.

This was demonstrated a few years ago when we were instructed to empty a modern detached house in Deganwy, owned by an elderly lady. Very much an everyday, routine call was how I had anticipated it, so off I went with keys in hand to see what needed to be done.

On entering the porch and hallway area of the house, I was confronted by a wall of knitting wool, brand new and still packeted and extending from the floor to the ceiling. 'Someone must like a bit of knitting,' was probably my initial reaction, until I proceeded to the lounge and living area. Just the same; packeted wool in all colours wherever I looked. It was exactly the same in the kitchen, by which time I had already anticipated the identical scenario throughout the first-floor bedrooms and bathroom. I was right, wool literally everywhere.

The contents of the house had to be disposed of in order to market the property. The wool, despite its vast quantity, actually sold very well. But it was very sad to think that so much of one product had not been happily and knowingly collected by the lady owner. Instead it had been accumulated as the result of some form of obsessive illness, of which, no doubt she would have been unaware.

I have come across clients on many occasions who have had, what I can only describe, again in lay person terms, as, 'cannot-throw-anything-away syndrome.' Deganwy was again the location of a very desirable property in an equally desirable area which I was asked to look at with the object of clearing.

I entered the house via the impressive front entrance and could proceed no further than about half a metre into the hallway due to a vast accumulation of newspapers dating back years and years, heaped haphazardly on the floors to about knee height. They were obviously easy to clear from the house despite the vast quantity, but it was sad to contemplate how, and why, they had got there in the first place.

My final, sombre reflection on the subject of 'collecting'

does not actually come within the realms of collecting at all. The resultant financial misery can be exactly the same though.

This is the phenomenon, or 'pastime' depending on one's viewpoint, known, I think, by the name of 'TV Shopping'. This is where folk sit in the comfort of their own homes, presumably with credit card at the ready, and purchase all manner of enticing health, household and DIY gadgets all attractively shown on screen by some well versed boy-or girl-next-door types.

The results can be frightening; I know of a lady whose elderly mother-in-law in Lancashire was found by her family to have spent £22,000 on television shopping. On being confronted by members of the family, she told them all to mind their own business, as her money was her own to do just as she wished!

In 2011 we were instructed to help clear surplus contents of a property owned by an elderly gentleman living alone in the Rhyl area. He was in the process of moving to residential accommodation. On entering the property, it became immediately obvious that the gentleman was an established television shopper. There were parcels, small and large, all over the house and the saddest feature was the fact that fewer than about five per cent of the parcels had been opened by the recipient. Many of the gadgets were of the gardening variety, but what an 82-year old widower with a very small garden was intending to do with them all had to be the subject of some speculation. Some of the kitchen items he had ordered would have made any trendy, newly-wed young housewife very proud to own!

The tragi-comic sequel to this anecdote is that some three weeks after settling in at the residential home, the elderly client ordered, and had delivered, via television shopping, a brand new electric hedge trimmer.

Little Coincidences

I often wonder how many of us at some time or another have experienced a 'coincidence' in our daily lives, often of little initial significance, but enough to cause us afterwards to exclaim, "How scary was that?"

I was born in Prestatyn in 1942, where we lived in a rented house whilst my father served his country in the RAF. He was stationed in the Azores in the North Atlantic where his task in the meteorological section was to compile weather reports for transmission back to the UK for the benefit of allied aircrew.

Since commencing business in Colwyn Bay, Prestatyn and its environs have very much been on my regular 'patch' as far as calls to private households are concerned in order to carry out valuations for a variety of purposes. Some years ago I determined that on my next visit to Prestatyn I would seek out my first home in Linden Walk and pay the present owner a surprise call, hoping not to cause undue inconvenience. I was able to identify only certain small features of the house from a photograph in my possession of 'yours truly' sitting up in his pram at 18-months old, outside the front door of the property.

I knocked on the door which was answered by an elderly gentleman who gave me a very cordial welcome, on being informed that I had been the occupier of the house all those 65 years or so ago. As I proceeded to refer to my father's wartime occupation in the Azores, he stopped me stone dead in my tracks and asked me to repeat what I had just said with regard to the compilation of the Atlantic weather reports.

"I can scarcely believe what you are telling me. Have you any idea what my wartime service duties were? I was stationed in North Yorkshire (he named a country house near Malton which had been requisitioned for the war effort) and you won't believe it, but my prime duties were to assimilate the weather reports sent to us daily, by, you've guessed it, our colleagues in the Azores!"

For a brief moment, we stared at one another, both of us, I suspect, thinking, "How scary is that?"

On a routine run of calls to Anglesey one day, my first call was to carry out a probate valuation of the effects of a deceased, retired vicar. Amongst chattels to be valued was his motor car, a Volkswagen Bora saloon, by then a model out of production. My very next pre-planned call was to a gentleman a few miles away who, on being introduced to him, I discovered was also a vicar whose motor car standing proudly by the front door was, to my great surprise – a Volkswagen Bora motor car.

I'd heard of 'Vicars and Tarts' but never 'Vicars and Boras!'

I was cataloguing some paintings at the saleroom one day; one of them was a watercolour by an artist called Ethelbert White. This particular work had appeared in a Royal Academy Exhibition in 1970, a label on the back of the work telling the full story as well as the name and address of the purchaser of the painting. That purchaser was a Mr Neale, whose address on the label was the house in Deganwy bang opposite the property Margaret and I had moved into just a few months previously.

Not particularly 'scary' as such, but quite a coincidence, I felt at the time.

20th Century Technology and Beyond

When Margaret and I commenced business in Colwyn Bay in 1992, one of our first equipment acquisitions was a second-hand word processor. This was used to input the catalogue details of all our forthcoming auctions. But that is just about all that went on from a computerised aspect.

Other vital details such as customer sale accounts and vendor statements were laboriously hand written for each and every sale. As we had been lucky enough to 'hit the ground running' right from the outset, three auctions every month were being processed in this biro-consuming way.

Every month, our own antique catalogue would be 'home-processed', a thoroughly laborious task but helped somewhat by our living on the premises in the flat above the saleroom. Thus 'popping to the office' usually took about eighteen seconds in our ancient lift; this journey was carried out regularly throughout the day.

Computer packages for auctioneers twenty-one years ago, were very much in their infancy apart from the fact that we felt ourselves to be, at that early stage, in a 'walk before you run situation' financially.

Eventually, however, we were put in touch, by whom I cannot recall, with a young, ambitious 'computer whizz' living locally. If James Elson knew very little about the auction business, he made up for it amply with his computer knowledge and sheer 'can do' attitude.

We more or less had to explain, in order of occurrence, every detail concerning the running of an auction to James. He, I seem to recall, had never attended a public auction, but was a quick and eager learner and very soon presented us with an impressive computer package prototype for us to assess.

With very little tweaking, James' system was accepted and installed, whereupon we were able to truly state that we were a computerised operation, albeit with certain major limitations. The next progress notch involved the sending via FAX of the draft catalogue to an intermediary in Chester who, following some weekend tweaking would then forward the final document to printers in Liverpool. Within twenty-four hours, 300 catalogues would be delivered to the saleroom spot on time every month.

This routine went on for many years in the 1990s and, indeed, so polished had we become in handling the process that Margaret and I actually paid a visit to Hong Kong for a five-day break in between two Tuesday auctions. On reflection, to have relied as we did on the time-keeping qualities of Cathay Pacific was somewhat rash, bearing in mind that, had we been delayed, there would not have been a replacement auctioneer for DRJ nor, indeed, an auction at all on that second Tuesday.

On the day of the auction I was not sure whether I was conducting it in Welsh, English or Cantonese!

Soon, those time-consuming limitations became major ones, so that the next, somewhat inevitable, step up for us was a computer package dedicated to the auction business. Nowadays, these appear to be the norm for most UK auction houses, although I do seem to recall that livestock auction packages were on the scene well before the fine art versions.

An important part of an antique auction is our responses to requests from all parts of the world, for 'condition reports' on items appearing in a forthcoming auction. Twenty years ago, those requests were made by telephone and we answered them, with as much detail as possible – by telephone. Wind on quickly to 2014 and those very same condition requests will be transmitted to us electronically (e-mail) and will receive an instantaneous reply, from us, accompanied by as many photo images as the client may require, again via the e-mail process.

Until comparatively recently, there were three methods by which an interested buyer could bid at an auction; in person at the auction (1), by leaving a written maximum bid (2) and by bidding on the telephone as the lot was being offered (3). These well-used processes were exactly as practised when I started all those years ago in Bangor.

There are no prizes for guessing that technology has once again taken a hand in adding a fourth method of bidding at a public auction. Please welcome 'Live Bidding' to the auction scene.

In very basic terms, live bidding means that a potential buyer, armed simply with a decent computer can locate him, or herself, in any part of the globe and bid on a lot as the auction is in live progress. No, there are absolutely no limits; you could be in the bath (waterproof laptop essential), on a patio sun lounger with gin and tonic in hand, on a cruise liner in the Carribean or even in the fruit & veg. section of M&S!

This last scenario is in fact, practised regularly by one of our locally-based lady customers, a very good buyer of quality English pottery, who finds the live bidding system ideal if she needs to shop and cannot spare the time to spend the whole of an afternoon at an auction waiting for just a couple of lots to come up.

As an 'oldie', I do confess to being fully supportive, and in total awe, of all the technological innovations which are now the commonest features in all facets of business today. In the unlikely event of my still being on that rostrum in a few years' time, with all this technology, and doubtless with lots more to come, there is the distinct possibility that I could be there with no one, absolutely no one, sitting in front of me in that saleroom on a sale day.

What a scenario to have to contemplate! It could even involve me in recalling those Thespian talents of long ago!

Documents For Sale

As a bit of a nostalgia buff, with old letter and billheads a particular source of interest, I am always more than a little keen when any form of old documentation presents itself for sale by auction. Any interest for me is always more from the historical, rather than from the monetary viewpoint, but at the same time having due regard for the interests of the seller who, quite naturally, will be looking to get the best price possible.

Some five years ago, a lady from Bangor invited me to take a look at what she, at the time, described to me, simply, as an 'old plan' she was keen to sell if the price were right. On inspection, I could scarcely believe the contents of this plan. Firstly, the lady was totally unaware that I was a member, and had been then for sixteen years, of Conwy (Caernarfonshire) Golf Club and that her plan dealt exclusively with the very large tract of land which is now the championship links course at Conwy.

Superbly drawn and coloured as long ago as 1860, the plan features detailed proposals for the residential development of the whole of the links area, now occupied by the golf course, and extending as far as the London to Holyhead railway line and the old main road leading out of Conwy. Two to three hundred properties were proposed, complete with tree-lined 'carriage drives'. The comprehensive details could so easily have been drawn up by one of today's major residential developers.

The map is very grandly entitled: 'Map of a Portion of the Conway Suburbs, the Property of the Corporation as laid out in lots for the erection of Victorian Residences 1860'.

Some patient research did not achieve the result I wanted. By 1877, seventeen years after the completion of this brilliantly drawn-up plan, there was little sign of its proposals being implemented. One cannot avoid the conclusion that finance, or the lack of it, was probably the final barrier to what would have been a very major development indeed for that period.

In this case, the 'what if' scenario is quite intriguing to contemplate. Firstly, we would presumably now be left with a very large estate of Edwardian villa-style residences in well maintained or run-down condition, who knows? Certainly, in today's estate agents' jargon, some would be described as having a 'superb waterfront location.'

Secondly, the very large detachment of the British Army would not have been able to occupy the land as a training camp prior to the First World War (traces of parts of the camp are still clearly visible on the golf course).

Thirdly, and here I display total bias, the land would not be what is now a much-loved and much heralded championship golf course which has been graced by very many famous personalities of the sport over very many years. The Club celebrated its centenary in 1995.

As to the actual sale of the plan: it duly came up for auction and I was authorised by the Club to bid on its behalf up to £100, if I recall correctly. Even keener buyers, in the form of the National Library of Wales, were the successful bidders at a rather higher figure, which ensured one very satisfied lady client.

For the golf club, however, there was also a very happy outcome. The National Library, always the ready helper, produced, and donated, an excellent, professional copy of the plan which now hangs proudly in the clubhouse for all to enjoy.

With regard to Conwy Golf Club, I wonder how many people are aware of the fact that in 1932, the famous British airwoman Amy Johnson tried to land her biplane, Gypsy Moth, on the course. It seems that the flyer, conqueror of the Cape, Tokyo and Australia with her exploits, was defeated on this particular occasion by the winds of Conwy. She ended her journey instead at Rhos On Sea, along with her flyer-husband Jim Mollinson, whose aunt lived in Conwy.

A well-known stalwart and life member of Conwy Golf Club, sprightly 87-year old Gordon Bennett, born and bred just outside the town near Oakwood Park, remembers vividly Amy Johnson's attempts to land her plane on that day. Determined to obtain the famous flyer's autograph, Gordon did so by following her to Rhos On Sea, whereupon she duly obliged!

Animal Magic

In January 2013, a bailiff acting on behalf of a debt collecting agency walked into the saleroom and plonked down in front of me what appeared to be a well-worn office ledger. The inevitable question was asked, "What do you think of this?"

'This' was, indeed, a rather scruffy, heavy and nondescript Twinlock file, weighing a hefty eleven pounds and whose surprising title read: 'Register of Animals Held at Belle Vue Zoo, Manchester, circa 1932 to 1967.'

On thumbing quickly through the first two or three pages, I immediately felt so grateful that this heavy tome was of pre-word processor vintage, and was hand-written from start to finish in fountain pen and even pencil, dependant presumably on who at a particular time had been inputting further details.

Those details were absolutely fascinating. Firstly, the whole ledger was sub-divided into the various types and species. Each stock, or zoo 'member', then had full details under various headings – birth date, sex, name, species type, state of health, illnesses with remedies proferred, date of death and if due to natural causes or for other reasons.

Some of those reasons were hilariously referred to, such as 'senile decay', 'thrown out of pouch' (some poor wallaby), 'overfed by public' and in the case of twenty-four grass snakes which met their end in 1961, 'for feeding to cobra'.

There were numerous and interesting references to financial transactions in respect of animals sold to Chipperfield's Circus, the Blackpool Tower Circus and also, to our very own Colwyn Bay Mountain Zoo.

One of the oldest Belle Vue inhabitants was Nicholas the hippo who arrived in 1938. Valued at £500 (£25 for each of his twenty years' life expectancy), Nicholas died suddenly in 1967. Yvonne was one of six elephants who arrived in 1939 and remained as a long-term resident until 1962. Robert was one of Belle Vue's first chimpanzees but was adjudged 'to be too old to train'.

'Unique' is a word rather freely over-used in our 'hard-sell climate' but in this instance, we were certain that its use to describe the Belle Vue ledger would not be deemed over the top.

Interest in the lot came from all quarters of the UK, some from unlikely sources, and soon our admittedly 'shot in the dark' estimate of £100 to £200 proved to be very much on the tentative side. 'Unique' lots are always the most difficult to place a value on.

The ledger was sold for a more than satisfactory £1400, the buyer, very appropriately, a zoological researcher from the Home Counties for whom, quite possibly, it will prove, very shortly, to be the bargain of the century.

Saucy Postcards

I refer fondly under this heading, to a consignment of, as new, 'saucy' postcards which came in for sale in July 2004. They had been entered by a very likeable young entrepreneur from Llandudno, Peter Heath. Peter was a keen 'dabbler' who scoured fairs, boot sales and auctions for a bargain for which he had a very keen eye.

This keen eye had taken him, as I recall, to a long-since closed down toy and gift shop in Llandudno, part of whose stock had been discarded only to gather dust in a forgotten part of the shop premises. Peter had spotted amongst those dusty treasures around 500 World War II coloured postcards, stored in boxes, all cleverly printed and coloured by one of the foremost publishers of seaside holiday postcards, A J Bamforth of Holmfirth in Yorkshire.

It was a lovely experience to thumb through what was a gentle taste of seaside innuendo humour seen, no doubt as a gentle pick-me-up during a period when the populace had war, poverty and austerity constantly on their minds.

Collectors from all over the country had shown keen interest in the cards which were offered as one lot, although there were duplicates of some of them. They say 'you cannot have it both ways,' and so it was with Peter's cards. Some interested bidders were bowled over by the new condition of the cards. Others were of the view that addresses and messages on the backs would have been preferable. I know, and care not. I was just pleased for Peter Heath that his 'eye for a bargain' brought him in a nice £1050 on the day.

Sadly, this promising and likeable young man with a talent for the old and unusual did not live to be able to fulfill that talent. He passed away from cancer not long afterwards, leaving behind a young family.

Found in an Oven
In September 2010, the national charity Age UK contacted us to ask if we were interested in taking on the emptying of the contents of a semi-detached house in Penrhyn Bay which had been bequeathed to it by the late Arthur Henry Stamp. This charity's nearest, regularly used auctioneers, were located somewhere down in England and promptly deemed Penrhyn Bay to be uneconomical, due to the distance involved, to take on the task. Their loss was to prove our gain.

Arthur Henry Stamp, by profession, was a teacher born in Penrhyn Bay, and attended Rydal School in Colwyn Bay. Oxbridge followed and he was duly awarded a BA and MA, both with Honours, and a PHD. He was a Fellow of several very prominent associations and societies in the United Kingdom.

In addition to his role as a writer and researcher (in 1996 he wrote a 620-page book, 'Penrhyn Bay, Its Story'),one of his former pupils described him, lovingly, as a teacher, lecturer, archaeologist, naturalist, philatelist, historian, government advisor, palaeontologist and private museum curator. Phew!

Other former pupils fondly described him as an 'absolute master of animation in the classroom'; his use of all manner of props to illustrate a point was, apparently, legendary, and they loved him for it.

The time came to pay a visit to Dr Stamp's unprepossessing semi-detached house in Penrhyn Bay, so along I went. I can only describe rather ineloquently, what met my eyes as I entered the house, was a wonderfully shambolic and very large assemblage of just about anything and everything one might expect to be associated with a person of such wide interests and talents.

I recall that it was probably easier to list in one's mind what there wasn't in the house as opposed to what there was such was the extent and variety of items displayed! Having taken a good overview of the contents I then had the actual removal logistics to assess and evaluate.

I eventually formed in my mind how I would approach the task and in what order of priority. As I was shortly due to depart on holiday, I decided to ask Ben, my younger son and one of the partners in the business, to pay his own independent visit to Dr Stamp's house to assess for himself the situation in order to compare our respective plans for the task ahead.

Departing on holiday, little did I realise the extent of the drama I had left behind. On my return from a most enjoyable break, the first words from Ben which greeted me were: "Have you heard of the excitement at Dr Stamp's in Penrhyn Bay?" My immediate reaction was to say "Of course not, I've been away", not realising that the headlines which had broken out in many newspapers and on television, could, quite easily have reached me anywhere, such was the excitement which had been generated in my absence.

Ben, as planned had paid his own assessment visit to Penrhyn Bay. 'Poking and probing', as one does during such visits, he just happened to open an old, well-past-its-sell-by-date, cupboard containing, to his utter shock and disbelief a grenade, a mortar bomb and, oh, just for good measure a German gas canister. Amazing, perhaps to behold, but the scenario was possibly not quite so surprising when one recalls the sheer extent and variety of Dr Arthur Stamp's eclectic collection!

The police were called and sirens wailed in Penrhyn Bay as an Army Bomb Disposal squad arrived to do its duty. Neighbours about to settle down to some routine daytime television viewing and some quiet knitting were told, not asked, to change their plans as quickly as possible and head off to do some unscheduled shopping in Llandudno and not to rush to return! So much for 'routine'!

Normality in due course returned to the area and what followed, one has to admit, was a good bit of free publicity for the Company with all the excitement which the cupboard contents had generated. Apparently, in a scenario such as this, neither the parties involved, nor members of the public, are told by the military whether the discovered items were actually live or not. Eccentric he may have been, but it is difficult to conceive that Dr Stamp would have knowingly harboured live ammunition at his home in Penrhyn Bay – but who are we to speculate?

And the surprises did not quite end right there. There was only ever going to be one destination for Dr Stamp's ancient gas cooker – the local recycling tip – which our removers were on the point of visiting as part of the total clearance of the property. Purely on a sudden whim, a quick, final inspection of the inside of the oven was decided upon just in case it contained an old, uneaten beef dinner or something. Well you can never be too vigilant. There was no beef dinner of the conventional kind but partly hidden on a shelf towards the back of the oven was a 'beef dinner' of the most valuable and unexpected sort – a plate of gold ingots, yes, solid gold ingots accompanied by a nice side-order of gold sovereigns and half-sovereigns which the eccentric doctor had squirrelled away for safe keeping. They all realised a cool £3,700 at the auction.

170 widely-varying artefacts comprised approximately one third of the entry for our Antique Auction on 28th September 2010 under the heading 'The Eccentric Collection of Dr A H Stamp (Dec'd) of Penrhyn Bay. They included handcuffs, neolithic arrows, a cat o'nine tails, torture instruments, a Victorian ear trumpet, a glass wasp-catcher, a Roman brothel token, iron keys (one labelled 'Dartmoor Prison'), a Georgian insanity recovery medal, skulls and antlers, Roman brooches and gaming devices, military swords and rapiers, Third Reich items, a 1795 handwritten livestock inventory, two suffragette newspapers, and there was more, a lot more.

It all added up to a very healthy £20,000 for Age UK due to the direct generosity of a gentleman who lived life to the very full, to the great benefit of all who came into contact with him. It was a great pleasure for us as a company to have been involved in such an interesting project. Thank you, Dr Arthur Stamp!

Beatlemania

Way back in the early 60s, I used to pay once-weekly visits to the Liverpool College of Commerce, for lectures in business and law given by an eminent member of the Bar. There would be lecture sessions both in the morning and the afternoon with a decent break for lunch in between. What I, and my fellow country bumpkins from over the border, found hard to understand was the absolute speed and urgency with which our fellow pupils disappeared out of the lecture room the very second that the bell was rung at lunchtime. On asking one of the locals where they all disappeared to with such rapidity, it was almost with incredulity that we were given the simple answer – "to The Cavern, of course".

Some fifty years on, there are few of us who have not heard of the icon of all pop venues, The Cavern, immortalised by one of the world's most famous pop groups, The Beatles. Even as an 'oldie' I still enjoy Beatles music, but far more rewarding for me were the instructions I received in 2013 to sell by auction a huge collection of show business and sporting autographs accumulated by one person over a number of years.

That person was Richard 'Ricky' Astall, a disabled gentleman confined to a wheelchair, from Abergele and previously Llandudno, who had passed away in 1995. His absolute passion was the collecting of sporting, pop and show business autographs. He travelled all over North Wales and beyond to amass his collection. Being disabled, Ricky gained ready access to the head of stage door queues and soccer dressing rooms and had well co-ordinated friends who queued on his behalf also. What gave such a genuine feel to the collection was that the majority of autographs which he had secured personally were invariably signed 'To Ricky, all the best', or some similar greeting.

In 1963, the Beatles appeared in concert at the Odeon Theatre in Llandudno and, on that same tour, at one or two other venues along the North Wales coast. The result was that Ricky had accumulated fourteen signed black and white photographs of the Beatles, together with their signatures on a page of one of the twenty-four small autograph books also in his proud possession. There were further signatures of the 'Fab Four' on a page of a large loose-leaf album.

By 2013, some eighteen years after Ricky Astall's death, his widow, Mrs Joy Astall, decided that her late husband's wonderful collection had accumulated enough dust in the house and that it was time to put it up for public auction. We were obviously delighted to be given the instructions to sell and, thanks to Mrs Astall's ready and enthusiastic input, we were able to give the auction much pre-publicity, which, combined with our internet facilities, would ensure considerable pre-auction interest. This duly proved to be case on 28th May when there were bids lodged not only from all parts of the UK but from Australia and the USA also.

To our, and of course, Mrs Astall's great delight, the five principal lots of Beatles' items realised a cool and hefty £19,800, a wonderfully fitting tribute to the enthusiasm of a gentleman who refused to allow illness and disability to be any sort of barrier to his life-long collecting passion.

On the Buses

Buses, trams and trains are very much top of the tree when it comes to the favourite contents of an antique sale. There is always a good following at our saleroom when any of these categories appear. North Wales has always been a popular photographic location for railway steam; Llandudno and Colwyn Bay had their beloved tram service, and the number of bus and charabanc companies in the region could be the subject of lengthy tomes in their own right. And so it was with great delight that we were instructed, in May 2010, to deal with a fascinating and potentially valuable collection of photographic slides.

These were entered for sale by a Mr Gareth Nickels, following the death in 2000 of his 80-year old father, John Nickels, whose lifelong passion had been the history and photography of many of the area's charabanc and bus companies. Wirral-born John had settled down in Rhyl after the Second World War, where he continued to amass a superb collection of 600 negatives in pursuance of his beloved hobby.

Supplementing the negatives were models, postcards and old timetables all relating to the business of running buses by companies which few of us will have heard of. There were Rhyl's White Rose Motor Tours Company, Red Dragon of Denbigh, North Wales Silver Motors, Royal Red Sunshine Coaches of Llandudno and Llangoed Red Motors – all of which were, in time, acquired by Crosville Motor Services.

John Nickels' main interest, however, was the White Rose Company, founded in Rhyl in 1912 by the Brookes Brothers. They started by running charabancs to local beauty spots but grew quickly, the fleet comprising just under one hundred buses and coaches before they were taken over in 1930. The Company also owned tipper wagons, removal vans, ambulances and hearses.

A particularly interesting slide on offer showed a massive White Rose, single-deck, open vehicle that was nearly thirty feet long with forty seats and dual entrance. The saloon accommodated thirty-nine people in two compartments (smoking and non-smoking) with the fortieth person sitting next to the driver.

Another showed a White Rose advertising board which

exclaims: 'We lead where others try to follow'. One of the longest excursions on offer, to Barmouth, left at 10 a.m. Not far by today's standards, but on unsurfaced roads with pneumatic tyres, quite adventurous. And the fare? Fifteen shillings (75p) while the fare to nearby Colwyn Bay was three shillings, Llandudno eight shillings and Llangollen, eight shillings and sixpence.

Other slides from this wonderful collection featured the Caernarvon Motors fleet of buses lined up majestically like soldiers in the town's Castle Square. These carried passengers on scheduled services to such places as Bethel, Llanberis, Pwllheli and Beddgelert. Other companies in the collection were Pye's Motor Tours of Rhos On Sea and Walsh's Crimson Coaches.

On the designated auction viewing days, and on the Tuesday of the auction itself, the premises were pleasingly full of 'bus anoraks' from all parts of the UK, all fully appreciative of the quality and importance of a collection lovingly amassed by one far-seeing enthusiast – John Nickels.

After some fierce bidding, both in the saleroom and on the telephone, the collection was knocked down to a transport enthusiast from Oswestry for a very reasonable single fare costing £2,800.

Chinese E–Mails

I like the Chinese people. We have many of them as customers, not only from North Wales but from Canada, Shanghai and from many other regions of China. They are a serene and unfailingly polite race and always show willingness to help, particularly whenever we may have a simple translation query to sort out. One of our local restaurant proprietors is always ready to come to our rescue despite the language constraints.

If I had a single criticism of them, it would be their apparent, and I emphasise the word 'apparent', difficulty in fully embracing the numerous machinations and requirements of the British auction system.

To be fair, they are learning and improving all the time; it is more a case of 'needs must', as they increasingly become bigger and bigger players in the international art market. Perhaps it is their inherent gambling instincts that sometimes get in the way and cloud their judgment on important issues, I do not know.

It is common knowledge that the Chinese are now very, very active world-wide in attempting to retrieve valuable heritage artefacts located all over the universe, that they feel should be back in their homeland where they feel they belong.

I relate below details, as far as they can be remembered, of a triple-email exchange which went on not long ago, between our company and a Chinese purchaser of a lot in one of our monthly antique auctions. We had sold to him a relatively unimportant piece of early blue and white Chinese porcelain for which we had received, admirably promptly, the total payment of the sum owing to us. A few days later, an e-mail arrived from the purchaser worded as follows –

"I buy Lot 232 in your auction for £490. I want packing to Shanghai, how much you charge?"

We passed on the request to our man in the saleroom, Richard, an expert and a thoroughly meticulous 'wrapper and packer' who went about working out the cost of packing together with the fully insured carriage via Fedex from Colwyn Bay to Shanghai all in the space of about one week. Our e-mail followed:

'Thank you for your e-mail request. The total cost fully insured and delivered by Fedex will be £90. Please confirm acceptance and despatch monies to us as previously'.

To our surprise, back came the following e-mailed reply – 'I no pay £90. £90 to (sic) much. I only pay £35 please reply'.

We duly did reply but only after giving the matter tactical thought for forty-eight hours. This is how we responded to Shanghai:-

'We note you do not wish to pay £90 for despatch from Wales to Shanghai. No problem. Vase is safe here in Colwyn Bay. You are welcome to collect at any time to suit.'

Within a further forty-eight hours the sum of ninety British pounds was nestling safely in our Colwyn Bay bank without as much as a further murmur from Shanghai!

This was a typical example of post-auction exchanges which sometimes do come along to try one's patience. All sorts of factors such as language, lack of auction-practice understanding, geographical distances and simple differences in business attitudes, all add up to cause the occasional frustrating situations. They are soon resolved, but often take time which could be otherwise better spent.

But our Oriental friends are learning the ropes gradually, which gives one the confidence that Welsh/Chinese relationships can only continue to get better.

Television

Antiques and television are synonymous with one of the Nation's favourite programmes. The Antiques Roadshow (or 'AR') first hit our screens way back in the late 1970s and has been regular Sunday evening viewing for many thousands of us ever since. Today's venues for a series are almost invariably going to be one of the country's stately homes or a well-known college or ecclesiastical building.

The slickness of the presentation is as sharp as ever and the programme is able to call on a very wide selection of experienced and respected experts. A bonus for the viewer these days is the delectable Fiona Bruce as presenter, she being only the second lady to have fronted the spectacle since its inception.

Every edition of AR seems to produce either objects of mouth-watering value or others having a fantastic background story, or both. So much so that one wonders just how many hopeful folk turn up at each event with relatively mundane objects having little or no chance of being assessed, let alone filmed for the programme. To the viewer, the queues of hopefuls seem, sometimes, to stretch for miles.

AR is that classic example of an outside location programme which, to the viewer, comes up trumps, looking perfect, every time. But inevitably, there will have been 'retakes' which we, the public do not see, and with the experience and skills of the editor, a few hours' filming time will be reduced to the smooth one hour which comes onto our screens before our dinners on a Sunday evening.

A funny example of a 'retake' or, I should more correctly say, 'retakes' in the plural, occurred many years ago when AR visited Llandudno. The rather hilarious sequence was enough to try the patience of a television crew who, one would have thought, had seen it all before.

An elderly lady had come to the filming venue with a very old teapot which a friend with an expert eye had persuaded her could be worth a lot of money. The teapot had lain on her living room mantlepiece for many years and had been used as a bit of a dump for old receipts and bits of fairly unimportant paperwork. The rarity and potential value of the teapot immediately excited the resident valuation expert who quickly confirmed the previous opinion regarding its potential.

The filming paraphernalia was duly set up and the lady owner primed to relate, as fully as she could, all she knew regarding the teapot, how long in her possession, where it had come from and, most importantly, the assertion that she had always felt it to be a worthless piece having little or no value or merit. This latter snippet is the sort which the programme organisers and the viewers always love to hear.

Filming started, and the lady owner began to relate, in very confident tones, the story about her teapot and the finer points which the interviewer had primed her on and things were proceeding well. Until that is, the unmistakably harsh sounds of the bells of a fire engine travelling down the promenade, were clearly heard by all in the room. "Cut" was the immediate cry of the director, looking frustratingly at the teapot's owner. With great apologies, she was asked to repeat her story exactly as previously and was encouragingly told how excellent she had been during the first 'take'.

On went the cameras again and off went the lady, just as confidently as before, when, lo and behold, the demanding cries of a baby in an adjoining room halted the proceedings once again. There was yet a third 'take' which lasted only a few seconds due to a technicality, before the film crew and the lady embarked once again on a story which, by now, nearly everyone in the room had become extremely familiar with.

The tone in the lady's voice had, by now a slightly wearisome but quite an understandable edge to it and it was with a degree of obvious relief that the story of the teapot was finally completed and declared to be 'in the can'.

I have only one qualm about AR which has always rather irked me somewhat. It concerns what I feel to be the inconsistent way in which it places values on items brought to the resident experts for their assessments. It is not uncommon, in the same programme, for an owner to be informed that his/her item 'should realise at auction such and such a sum'. And for the next person to be informed that he/she 'should insure their item for such and such a sum'.

Now, human nature being what it is, such contradictory advice is going to lead to one thing only – confusion. Insurance and auction values are on two entirely different levels; insurance usually being the higher, and an owner is only going to hear one thing – the higher of any two figures quoted, after all, that is what he/she will have come to hear in the first place.

On many occasions I have had clients excitedly quoting potential values of items heard by them on AR because 'they have one just like that', only to have to be brought down to earth with the bad news that what they heard quoted last Sunday was a figure for potential insurance cover and not a valuation figure for sale on the open market.

By today, all those years on from the birth of AR, several other antique-related programmes regularly grace our screens, the public seemingly hungry for more and more of the knowledge which some of them impart. I say 'some of them', because in my humble opinion, there are programmes which undoubtedly entertain the viewer but which have little, or no resemblance to what actually happens in real life and which are so far removed from reality as to be quite laughable.

I fully admit to being totally biased in singing the praises of the BBC's '*Flog It*' series, which has visited us in Colwyn Bay on three occasions. More than any one of its rival programmes, '*Flog It*' shows it as it really is; you attend the valuation day with your precious treasures and if you like what you hear, and if the producer is keen to have them, you consign your items to the auction, following which, you pay commission in the usual way for the services of the auction house.

For the record, I often have to state, which comes as a huge surprise to those who ask, that, as an auction house, we do not receive a single penny, nor a euro either, for our appearances on '*Flog It*'. A fact I do not resent, as the publicity from the programme seems to do us no harm at all.

Social Changes

During the last ten years or so, the antiques world has experienced quite enormous changes in tastes and in the demands of the buying public. Values of some categories of items, coupled with a total falling-out of favour for others, have, quite simply plummeted; the end result has been to give the totally erroneous impression that antiques, across the board, have gone out of fashion. Nothing could be further from the truth.

When I began my career all those years ago, it was an accepted theory that three things were guaranteed to provide security and a cast-iron financial return – bricks and mortar, the stock market and antiques. By today, sadly, all those three have been through the 'old mill of uncertainty', with certain sectors of the antiques world experiencing their share of 'the wobbles'.

In terms of relatively everyday objects with which most of us will be familiar, such as cut glass, brass and copperware, electroplate, tea and dinner services and even the Welsh Dresser and the grandfather clock, all so beloved by us all, the demand for these – and consequently their value – has dropped considerably And the reason for this? In my humble opinion, a contributor to this situation has been the influence of, you might have guessed, television.

Not only has the 'telly' given endless entertainment to everyone on the antiques side, it has also infiltrated our lounges with programmes on how and where to buy property, how to alter and modernise the property once we've bought and finally, how to furnish the property in a style to which we are all totally unaccustomed! And of course, if the television tells us all how best, in its opinion, to follow a programme's advice, then, all of us, like lambs to the slaughter, do just that.

Another certain contributor to the changes in tastes which we have all been witness to, is twenty first century social attitudes and a commendable emphasis on equality in the domestic environment.

When I visit properties these days, I constantly find myself referring to items 'from the age of elegance,' often to the obvious surprise and disappointment of an owner.

'Tea' tables were just for that – having a nice cup of tea accompanied by postage stamp sized sandwiches with the crusts cut off and nice chat about a feathered bonnet recently purchased. 'Tea,' as such is no longer taken, particularly by the 'mod.young' in our society.

Neither do they put their boiled eggs on an electroplated stand resembling a fairground carousel. Nor biscuits in an elegant biscuit barrel, nor vegetables in plated entrée dishes, nor crumpets, of all things, in a lidded crumpet dish .... I could go on.

If, these days, the lady of the house needs a nice glass vase for her latest, ever-so-cheap bunch of supermarket flowers; not for her a high-quality cut glass example as used by Aunt Bertha, but a plain and simple one, beautifully made in the Czech Republic and costing little more than about £10.

And what about Aunt Bertha's lovely tea services all neatly stacked like soldiers in her beloved china cabinet? I'm sorry Aunt Bertha, but the dishwasher and the microwave now dictate our drinking and eating habits. And as for the decanting of a nice bottle of 'Aussie Red' into a quality piece of cut glass, forget it. Unscrew the top, 'cheers' and 'down the hatch' is now so often the norm!

No, the lady of the house has long ago laid down the 'laws on domestic task-sharing' – and who can blame her? If 'he' plays golf, then 'she' goes to pilates or the gym. Child-minding and school-collecting tasks are shared, and often the cooking duties too.

When it comes to furnishing the modern family home, today's young homeowners are more likely to visit a well-known Scandinavian furniture mega-store than an auction saleroom selling good quality, solid wood furniture with years of use ahead of it.

I also find that there is far less enthusiasm on the part of young homeowners to accommodate older antique items bequeathed to them by a deceased relative. I remember the situation years ago when 'Nain's Welsh Dresser' would be the first on the list of cherished family items to retain when Nain passed away.

No longer does that situation prevail. Television programmes have persuaded us that some of today's medium-sized, modern properties have not the space to accommodate a 6-foot long Welsh dresser with relatively limited storage space and restrictive height.

As recently as 2012, we sold a fine, small, 18th Century Merioneth Welsh Dresser for £3,500 on behalf of a lady having to sell as she was moving to a small apartment. Some ten years previously, we had valued the very same dresser at £8,000, but the lady, at that time, did not need to sell.

These are the realities which today go a long way to dictating the lifestyles of the modern family, not to mention the fortunes of many an auction house.

I am constantly being asked the question, 'Will we see the return to favour of brown furniture and good quality Edwardian and Victorian items?' I really am not so certain that we shall. The modern, light look is what the customers now seek, particularly those in the under-forty-five age bracket.

In our twice-monthly 'home contents' auctions, the sight

of a good few lots of well cared for Ercol, G-Plan or Ikea furniture present no problem at all, whereas a well-mellowed Edwardian sideboard with years of service to come will elicit barely a glance.

It's an interesting, but funny, old world, is it not?

Ladies of the Night

For some years now, in my capacity as an auctioneer, I have been invited to speak and give 'road shows' at branches of the *Merched y Wawr*, the Women's Institute and other organisations around the region. I admit that there have been occasions, after a hard day's work, when the last thing I'd wanted was to dash home for dinner followed by a fifteen-mile journey along country lanes to a 'ladies do' in a local community hall.

But there has never been a single occasion when I have really regretted agreeing to one of these events. A truly warm welcome is always guaranteed from membership numbers sometimes from as few as a dozen, or thirty or forty and, on rarer occasions fifty to sixty. There is always a *'paned'* (a cuppa') afterwards and, more often than not, custard creams and chocolate digestives.

The other thing I like is that all the ladies I see are good sports and fun-loving, always responsive to some leg-pulling and banter. But the one thing I am truly conscious of is the contribution they all make to the well-being and, often, the sheer survival of small, remotely-situated communities. My contribution is therefore minimal compared to the efforts they all put in.

On 10th of June 1993 I prepared myself after work to make my way to a WI meeting in Betws Y Coed at which I had agreed to give a talk.

At the time, Margaret and I were living in the flat above the saleroom. Making my way down the A55 towards the

Black Cat roundabout, I could not help observing the large quantities of water lying in the fields alongside the Expressway. It had been raining torrentially, non-stop, all day but it was not until I reached Glan Conwy and saw vast quantities of water gushing out of manholes in the middle of the road that I realised just how much water had fallen out of the skies on that day.

Luckily, I had allowed extra time to get to Betws, but it was still two hours later when a bedraggled yours truly arrived at a venue full of patient ladies. Remarkably, Betws had not received quite the same rainfall as down the valley, but the following morning's local and national newspapers all carried the dramatic pictures of what afterwards became known as the 'Llandudno Floods.'

Perhaps it is not altogether surprising that another 'road show' anecdote has the weather as its main subject. I had gone to give a talk, in the depths of winter, to a *Merched y Wawr* branch in a remote part of the Vale of Clwyd. Halfway through what was proving to be a funny and jolly evening, came rumblings from some of the ladies who had noticed through the schoolroom windows, evidence of heavy, falling snow.

In view of some remote and diverse areas which some of the ladies had to return to, it was decided to have an early *'paned'* and then bring proceedings to a close. All right so far, except when we all departed to our cars, none could be identified due to the covering of snow. Furthermore, it soon became obvious that getting the cars out of the sloping car park of the schoolroom was definitely not to be taken for granted.

Now, there were seven cars in that car park, with a passenger list of about thirteen ladies and also one man without passenger – yours truly – who took a little time to realise that, as the only person in a snowstorm at ten o'clock at night with a bit of muscle, it was going to be my task and no one else's to help get these ladies on their way home.

After a great deal of pushing and shoving, I eventually got each car on its way and with each departure there was a generous blowing of kisses and '*diolchs yn fawr*' (thankyous) in my direction. Job well done, I thought, as I proceeded, in quite self-satisfied mode and in total isolation by now, to my own vehicle and 'home James'.

There was only one slight problem – I could not, for the life of me, manoeuvre my vehicle out of the rather tight corner I had parked it in. All my ladies had disappeared into the night, so there was no help to be had there. In non-snow conditions, getting out would have been easy, but this was a different scenario as I began to contemplate not getting home for breakfast, never mind bed!

Suddenly, coming in the direction of the schoolroom, I heard the tipsy chatter of at least two men returning home from a good night out. I carefully made my way to the gateway to await their arrival and within a matter of minutes all of us had got the car onto the road ready for a long-awaited journey home.

The snow had fallen thickly on the minor lanes so that it was with very much care and lightness on the pedals that I eventually reached home after what had been intended as just a little roadshow chat with the ladies!

John Parry of Rossett

John Parry of Rossett is a name synonymous with two quite different activities. Firstly, John Parry became a builder of quality homes in and around the Chester and Wrexham areas in a period which rather preceded the mass-market building concept we are now so familiar with today.

Having abandoned plans to train as an accountant due to a serious injury, he embarked on a building career in 1965.

He borrowed £1000 to purchase his first JCB for £1600 and never really looked back, selling out in 1987 after a successful and lengthy career. But, typically of John, 'his builder's feet' soon became very itchy, so much so that he started a second building career in 1990 but finally sold out again in 2001, on realising that family members did not want to follow him in to the business.

In my own business, however, John's name became far more well-known throughout not only North Wales, but literally anywhere there was a good piece of antique furniture to be bought either by auction or via retail sources.

I'm not sure which of the two he regarded more as a business than as a hobby but for many years he very successfully wore two hats – that of high-class residential builder and that of aficionado and huge enthusiast for quality English and Welsh furniture. His countless number of forays to bid on, and buy, quality items knew no bounds.

John, in the 70s and 80s, was regarded as the scourge of so many of his rivals in the trade.

When John entered the Saleroom (as I remember his doing on many occasions in Gaerwen) there would be a discernible change of atmosphere, as glances between traders or dealers already there signalled a realisation that one of their most feared competitors had just entered the arena! He would wait for his chosen l ots to come up, make his bids and then depart as quickly as he had entered, leaving his fellow traders in his wake.

In 1997 John disposed of his first fantastic collection of furniture at a major auction in London. The catalogue for that auction has become, by today, a much sought-after term of reference.

Now in his late 70s having battled serious illness, John's exuberant enthusiasm for quality furniture persists in abundance, not for him a false admiration for something simply because 'it might be worth a bit of money'. His analysis of a piece goes much deeper – the grain, the colour and the quality of workmanship are all so important to him as demonstrated when he describes a piece as if it were a living thing or a close member of his family. When he talks about furniture, he simply gushes an enthusiasm which becomes totally infectious.

His success as a builder enabled him to finance high value purchases such as oak Welsh dressers at £50,000 and John would often spot important features in a piece which many might not. His keen eye and knowledge have proven even more important in a world where fakes, forgeries and reproductions can so easily catch the unwary out. John has also been a good judge and assessor of trends which are forever changing in this business, and readily concedes that his beloved early oak hasn't quite the same appeal in 2014 as it had in the recent past.

In 2010 John disposed of a second valuable collection of furniture, on his own admission not quite as successfully as the first, no doubt compounded by changing trends, tastes and lifestyles. His love of quality timbers such as walnut and yew, as well as oak, may well be the basis of yet a third collection and knowing John, this could be even more important. John continues to live and breathe fine furniture.

Talking to John Parry on the subject of quality antique furniture is akin to attending a lecture by an expert exuding the sort of enthusiasm which is the envy of most of us.

John Parry of Rossett is a class-act. Long may he continue!

Woolly Wills and Feuding Families
I fully realise that a 'woolly will' may well sound like a trendy nickname. For me, however, it is something I sometimes come across when carrying out valuations for probate

purposes. Far from being trendy, it can be troublesome, time-consuming and, in extreme cases can cause serious family rift.

A 'woolly will' is my term for describing a will (someone's Last Will and Testament) which has been drawn up in a slightly vague way omitting small, but vital, points thus leaving too many important details to open interpretation. Wills by their very nature are supposed to convey the exact, unequivocal wishes of the deceased person. Vagueness is not a good ingredient for that recipe.

A task I am often involved in is that of carrying out chattels valuations (furniture, valuables, home effects and, indeed technically, everything inside a property which the deceased person owned) on behalf of the administrator of an estate. Thankfully, most are perfectly straightforward and snag-free, but there are occasional exceptions which is where the time-consuming 'fun' starts.

Wills often contain, right at the beginning, what are known as 'specific bequests.' I have come across a few 'woolly wills' couched in terms such as 'I leave my cut-glass vase to my nephew John Bloggs.' Nothing wrong with that, very straightforward, you may think. Off to the property to carry out the valuation and to firstly seek out the specific bequests, including the 'cut glass vase' referred to. Ah, no problem, I tell myself as I spot one handsome cut glass vase standing proudly on the sideboard in the lounge. Put a valuation figure on it and proceed smartly through the rest of the house, dictating everything into one of these infuriating digital machines. But there, in the dining room facing me on a bookcase, yes, you've guessed it, another cut glass vase!

Now herein 'lieth a problem', as they say. The lounge cut glass vase is far, far superior in quality to that in the dining room but has a nasty chip in it, as opposed to the latter sample in pristine condition. Which cut glass vase was intended to be given to the nephew of the deceased? Mere guesswork in such a case is not really sufficiently scientific. The time-consuming possibilities or probables have then to be considered. Assume the better quality, albeit chipped, vase to be the one intended? Go for the less valuable, but perfect example? Or hedge one's bets and advise that both be given to nephew John and hope there are no repercussions?

All that would have been required to avoid all this would have been a slightly more elaborate reference to the bequest, such as – 'I leave my tall cut glass vase standing on the lounge sideboard to my nephew John Bloggs'. Simplicity itself, but if that is seen as a complication, how about this further example – 'I leave my 3-piece silver tea service to my niece Jane Bloggs'.

Again, on the face of it, no problem – except that the only 'silver' tea service present in the property is in fact, an electroplated one of substantially less monetary value and far removed in any case from being a solid silver one. Two scenarios present themselves in this instance. Either the deceased used the term 'silver' as a generic description (a common error), not fully realising the difference between the two, as they both look like 'silver' after all, or, and this is when the poor valuer, yours truly, has a real problem – there is, in fact, hidden away in this heavily furnished property full of dusty nick-nacks, a genuine, solid silver tea service which has long-since been squirrelled away by the owner for safe keeping.

Time now has to be spent (wasted more like), looking in every nook and cranny for another silver tea service which may never have existed in the first place!

Again the remedy to avoid this unfortunate scenario would have been some form of predetermination as to whether the 'silver' tea service, if the only one actually in the house, was in fact solid silver, or the inferior electroplate. A tip to the reader – look for the lion passsant on solid silver and for letters such as A1, EP or EPNS on electroplate. Also the marks on plate are generally far more detailed and complex than those on solid silver items.

Being precise and leaving nothing open to interpretation in a will is extremely important for one other vital reason – family harmony. For the death of a family member to be overshadowed by disharmony, often over the most trivial of objects, is very sad indeed.

A scenario I do encounter quite often is when a homeowner, with the kindest and best of intentions, has intended to leave items to friends and relatives just by sticking named labels or suchlike to the base of each piece with the innocent intention that those wishes be acted upon when the time came. Sadly, if those directions are not stipulated in a formal will, they have no validity in law. Most families in such cases acknowledge without a moment's dissent, the informal intentions of their loved ones. I have, however, encountered the very sad, albeit rare, occasions where one member in a family has challenged another's right to something simply because it was not formally directed in the will.

The saddest, and most extreme, outcome to this situation has occurred where dissenting factions in the same family have attended an auction to bid against one another for items which each faction believed should have been theirs, 'because Aunty Edna always said that we were to have them.'

Such a situation generates, at the very least, permanent rifts within, hitherto harmonious families, and, at worst, family matters and dirty linen being aired in a court of law.

There are never winners in such sad cases but we all

know how peculiar human nature can sometimes be!

It's the Good Life

Some 53 years on from that moment when my mother speculatively popped the question "How do you fancy being an auctioneer", I have to state, without hesitation, that it was the best question she ever asked of me. In today's jargon – I really have had a ball.

Monday mornings still arrive with that buzz of anticipation as to what I might come across between then and Friday afternoon. And it is a fact that I still come across items I have never seen examples of in all the time that I've been operating.

I have been exceedingly lucky too in one important aspect – good health. I calculate that since I commenced my career in 1960, my absenteeism from work due to relatively minor ailments, the worst of which was a broken wrist, totals three and a half weeks.

This profession is not the one for anyone who does not like meeting people on a regular basis. A very large and important part of our business model is that we are always keen to go out to visit clients in their homes in order to value items for potential sale, without their having to pack and load them to bring to the saleroom.

On the basis of a very conservative estimation of five visits per week for this purpose, as well as to carry out valuations for a variety of legal and insurance reasons, it is easily calculated that in the twenty-two years we have been operating in Colwyn Bay, I will have visited approximately 5,000 homes stretching from Aberdaron in the far west, via Anglesey to Hoylake in the far east and anywhere else south of those locations!

Those visits have revealed happiness, sadness, poverty – sometimes of an unimaginable degree – wealth, good taste, very bad taste, the worst that families can sometimes inflict on one another for the sake of a few possessions and, so importantly, a very great deal of human understanding and genuine kindness and humour, so inherent in the make-up of all of us in this country.

I have had well known sports personalities, politicians, theologians and a certain famous poet as clients. I have also had, and still have, all those ordinary Mrs Joneses, Mr Robertses, Mrs Williamses and Mr Hugheses as very faithful customers, some still with us after over twenty years of regular attendance. These are the people that the wise owl, Morgan Evans, referred to all those years ago – the so-called 'small' persons, who, if treated properly, will stay with you long after the 'big' customer has moved on to pursue some bigger fish.

Our two sons, John and Ben, are well established in the business, and the opening of an additional saleroom in our capital city, Cardiff in July 2013 has been a venture which has taken off very promisingly. I shall continue for just as long as I am able to be usefully involved.

My one hope is that they will get as much enjoyment and job satisfaction as I have had over so many years.

Who would want to be a bank manager?   Not I!!